THE BRITISH, EUROPEAN AND
AMERICAN SHORTHAIR CAT

The British, European and American Shorthair Cat

Phyllis Lauder

B. T. Batsford Ltd. London

Typeset in Alphatype Century Old Style 10 on 12 point
by Progress Filmsetting, Leonard Street, London
and printed in Great Britain by
Redwood Burn Ltd
Trowbridge and Esher
for the publishers B. T. Batsford Ltd.
4 Fitzhardinge Street London W1H 0AH

Contents

Temperament   Cats as pets   Showing household
pets   Feeding   Cats and children

List of Illustrations

Acknowledgments

The author and publishers would like to thank the following for their permission to reproduce the illustrations used in this book: Anne Cumbers (3, 5, 6, 8, 9, 16, 17, 18, 21, 24, 25); Derek Davis (23); Jane Hamilton (7); Glen Hellman (19); Mark Henrie (20); David Irwin (15); *Purr* (26); Sam L. Scheer (1); Pauline Stephens (10, 11, 12, 13); Hetty van Winsen (2, 4, 14)

1

Origins

Interest in cats has been, during the twentieth century, largely concentrated upon the breeding and fostering of exotic varieties such as Siamese and Burmese, and the spectacular Persians. So much has been written about these, and so many pictures of them have appeared, that it almost seems as though the sturdy domestic cat has faded into the background of the cat world. But in fact this is not the case: there are well-filled classes at important championship shows for the cats known in Britain as British shorthairs, in Europe as Européens, and in the United States as North American shorthairs or as domestic shorthairs, the name by which they are listed in the American Cat Association's standards.

Probably domestic shorthair is the best name for these cats, since they are to be found all over the world, and this name does not suggest that they are peculiar to any one country. It has to be remembered that *Felis domesticus* is, in some parts of the globe, a fairly recent immigrant. He was not indigenous to Australia and New Zealand; when man went across the sea from Malaya, there were only marsupials in these countries, and the much later coming of the white man saw also the arrival of the 'ship's cat', founder of the household pet cat population of the antipodes of today: '*F. domesticus* first came to Australia with Governor Phillips and the first fleet. More would have come with each shipload of settlers'.[1] There is in Australia an animal called the dyasure, partly a tree-dweller, who has been spoken of as a cat, and who likes birds' eggs; he is in fact a marsupial, the young being carried in a pouch, and he has no connection with the felidae.[2] The coming of the domestic cats to Australia was not without drawbacks: '... operations of farmers discourage other birds and animals that keep plagues in check; the foxes, cats and pigs that they introduced have created a rarity of ground-nesting birds'.[3] The plague in question concerned locusts, which the ground-nesting birds ate, so that their destruction by the farmers' imports gave the locusts free rein.

Felis domesticus is not, either, native to America. There is little doubt that man's ancestors traversed the ancient land-bridge which is now the Bering Strait to become the remote forebears of the American Indians; but when Columbus crossed the Atlantic, there were no horses in America, and no cats either. It should be remembered that the separation of the land masses of Africa and America by the ocean had occurred long before the appearance on earth of the first cats.[4] It may, in fact, be accepted that the Spaniards, who took the horse with them to the New World in the late fifteenth and early sixteenth centuries, took also the cat.

It is sometimes said that the North American shorthair is the 'original' cat, and this indeed is true in the sense that he is the present representative of the cats who came from the Old World four centuries ago and who were descendants of earth's first domestic cats; but though it is plain that the North American shorthair represents, as a direct descendant, the species *Felis domesticus,* he did not orginate on American soil, but came along with the white man and the horse. Incidentally, horses and cats have always been friends in some measure. In the days—not so very long ago—when motor-cars were thin on the ground, and there was stabling in town and country, there was nearly always also a stable cat. This would be a 'moggie' and, almost invariably, a domestic shorthair. And if the cat was a female and there were kittens enjoying mock battles in the stable yard, you could see a horse who intended to take step backwards turning his head to make sure that in retreating he would not tread on the new arrivals.

It has never been possible to say precisely when *Felis domesticus* made his appearance among terrestrial fauna; earliest records are from ancient Egypt, but when these records were made, the cat had doubtless already existed for millennia: dying above ground, he left no fossil remains; but he probably shared man's caves during a long prehistory, and we may hazard an informed guess that he was a short-haired animal of more-or-less rounded type, and with colouring of a wild-type pattern approximating to agouti or to some sort of tabby, or possibly tending towards the 'speckled' fur which the Cat Fancy of today knows as Abyssinian.

It has been claimed that the first recorded cats were long-headed, but this is not always borne out by the facts. The claim is based upon mummies in tombs and upon ancient Egyptian representations in stone: the cats were etched in a sort of bas-relief, and represented in profile, and these carvings show some length of head. The carved pictures are of a conventional style; they were made something like six millennia ago and evolution is not static: there must have been alterations in life forms during so long a period. It is probable that the cats of ancient north Africa were different from the cats of today: 'Morrison-Scott (1951) has shown that the average skull size of mummified Egyptian cats is significantly larger than that of the cats of today'.[5] However, more recent cats of eastern provenance have not shown long heads: in the 1930s and 40s there was, at the Natural History Museum in London, a stuffed Siamese cat, and this animal's head was 'as round as an apple' to quote one of England's prominent experimental breeders, the late B. A. Stirling-Webb. The taxidermist's work showed a large cat of strictly 'domestic' type. In fact, the exhibition shorthairs of today have even rounder faces than had the sidewalk moggies of the early 1900s from whom they were bred.

The domestic cat is eminently fitted for survival. He is able to fend for himself by eating the rats, voles, rabbits and — alas! — birds that he catches; equipped with strong teeth and claws to fight his enemies and to escape, by climbing trees, from his predators; and, above all, dowered with the ability to please and charm man. This last characteristic might well have stood him in good stead during prehistoric days, for no doubt palaeolithic man was happy to see vermin chased from his food stores and rubbish dumps, and willing to allow the small, friendly destroyer of rats a place by his fire or shelter in his cave. Whether this was or was not the case, it is certain that the cat was loved by man in later times: recorded history shows him honoured even as a god, in Egypt and, much later, greatly loved in Europe.

As he has evolved man has shown, in various ways, extreme cruelty; and his domestic animals have suffered in ways that are horrifying to people of today. Some of the worst cruelties that the cat ever suffered were inflicted in the name of a gentle, beautiful religion, when, as some poor old beldame was burned at the stake for a witch, her cat, stigmatised as her 'familiar spirit', endured a frightful death with her. We have to remind ourselves that the people of those days really believed that the cat concerned was a minor devil.

However, bad times though they have been through as a race cats have triumphantly survived earth's cataclysms and man's stupid cruelty. By and large, man has loved the cat. From the monastic poet's Pangur Baṇ to Dr Johnson's Hodge, learned folk have appreciated him, and through good times and bad, the cat has never lost his independence. He has, in fact, exploited man to the top of his bent, taking all that he needs, and giving nothing in return! Probably his skill in keeping down vermin can be accounted a payment for the food and shelter that he takes as of right; certainly his beauty, his cleanliness and his cajoling, purring ways have endeared him to his protector. In recent centuries, both famous people and humble cottagers have welcomed cats to their homes, and provided them with food and warmth, and with leave to rear their kittens in the towns and farmlands of Europe and America.

It was not until the end of the nineteenth century that the Cat Fancy came into being. Its early beginnings in Britain are described by a ship's doctor, who was also a veterinary surgeon, writing circa 1872.[6] Doctor Stables lists the classes at what he refers to as 'pussy shows' taking place at the Crystal Palace and at Birmingham. It is barely a century since his book was written, but there is an enormous difference between the thinking of the cat-lover of today and his counterpart of a hundred years ago; and the ideas of this author, in his own time very knowledgeable in matters concerning the cat, must seem curious, and even laughable, to the fancier of the 1980s.

In his list of the classes at the Crystal Palace and Birmingham shows, Dr Stables discusses the points to be looked for in the exhibits. As to shorthairs, he starts off cheerfully with 'Class 1. And first on the list comes *Tortoiseshell Tom*'. He finds Tortoiseshell Tom an ugly feline, and expresses surprise that he has only seen one, who died at three months old. In many of the classes listed, the exhibits are to be judged by 'size', and he observes that the *Black and White* '...is a large, handsome, gentlemanlike fellow...'. Dr Stables has unusual advice to offer to exhibitors in the matter of preparing an exhibit's coat for the show: he advocates putting little dabs of fresh cream here and there over the cat's fur, upon which, he says, the prospective contender will wash his coat so thoroughly and so extensively as to produce a beautiful, shining pelage! His chapter on ailments, too, reads oddly to modern eyes; he tells his readers that if a cat should have a convulsion, a smelling-salts bottle should be held to his nostrils, or a pinch of dry snuff and, if this does no good, 'Pussy must be bled'.

Although, however, the fancier of today can smile wryly at this century-old book, its author has a great understanding of the cats that he so obviously loved: he understands, as few did in his day, and some do not even today, that a cat will not make a good hunter unless he is well-fed, since a half-starved cat will not have the strength and energy to pursue and deal with prey. He knows that cats need water to drink. He rages at the cruelty sometimes inflicted upon cats by selfish, stupid people. He devotes a chapter to calling for 'parliamentary protection for the domestic cat', stating that 'laws have been framed for the good of horses, dogs and game; nay, even the very wild birds of the field have their friends in Parliament; but the poor cat is left out in the cold'. Gordon Stables, indeed, was a pioneer; he and his like were first to promote the appreciation of the cat which started with books of this kind and with exhibitions for cats at such shows as the one in Birmingham, which had many sections, including one for dogs. Their interest and enthusiasm was a beginning, which led, a little later, to that of the great names of the turn of the century: Lady Marcus Beresford, and Mrs Clinton-Locke of Chicago; in fact, to the people who inaugurated the golden age of twentieth-century admiration and understanding of cats.

During the present century, a great deal of new knowlege has come to man, and the cat, appreciated as never before since he was worshipped in Egypt, has shared in the benefits which science can confer. It almost seems as though the wheel of scientific progress has been given an extra twist, to make it spin faster, and even the frightful wars which humanity inflicted upon the world brought, as wars always do, an upsurge of inventiveness and of research which, intended to protect by the destruction of enemies, provided also some benefits. Today, medical knowledge has made such strides that the notion of bleeding a patient seems antediluvian; and research into feline ills carried out in splendidly-equipped laboratories has brought immunisation from conditions formerly fatal, for any cat whose owner will pay for his cat's safety.

Nowadays most children can discuss DNA intelligently; but nothing at all was known of genetics in the 1800s; for Gregor Mendel's work was not acknowledged nor published until 1900 — after the death of the brilliant scientist who, trying for a degree, was failed for 'Lack of insight and insufficient knowledge![7]

Dr Stables, writing in the 1870s, could not have known anything about dominance or the sex-linkage of yellow in the cat, and so could not understand the scarcity or the vulnerability of 'Tortoiseshell Tom'!

Today, cats are protected in many ways, and Gordon Stables, crying out for parliamentary legislation for them, was one of those who brought into being the much-needed protection. It was not, in his time, realised that it is impossible to license cats as dogs are licensed; governing bodies have carefully considered the question, and have not found the idea of licensing to be practical politics. For if all cat-owners had, by law, to take out a licence—as is done in the case of dogs—not only would many cats immediately be put to sleep by owners unwilling to pay the price of a licence, but it would be found almost impossible to enforce the law. Such a law would imply registration, and identification, probably with the wearing of a collar with the owner's address. The usefulness of such identification is that if an animal is lost or abandoned or stolen, the police may take him to a shelter where he will be fed and housed while his owners are contacted or, if he has been abandoned, where he may be put to sleep if no home is available for him. Presumably the police would also be able to impound any cat found not wearing a collar. But how could anyone catch a cat who did not want to be caught? Approach him, and the hedge stirs, and there is no cat.... Besides, such legislation would almost certainly result in wholesale misery for countless strays turned out by unscrupulous persons not willing to license them.

Nevertheless, the cat is now legally protected: in British law (Animal Protection Act 1911) *a cat is a domestic animal.* And 'Where a person who has been convicted of an offence of cruelty is again so convicted the court has power...to order his disqualification from having custody of any animal or any animal of a specified kind'.[8] 'It is an offence for the owner...of an animal to abandon it...the punishment is a fine not exceeding £50 or imprisonment up to three months or both'.[9] Under the Larceny Act 1916 'All animals that have value and are the property of any person are larcenable'.

Thus, the cat can claim legal protection; and he has also the help of the Royal Society for the Prevention of Cruelty to Animals, whose officers will deal with cases that come under the various Acts if these are reported to them. There is also the International Society for the Prevention of Cruelty to Animals, with headquarters in Boston, Massachusetts. The splendid Cats' Protection League, too, affords help to any and every cat who needs it. For addresses, see Chapter 11, page 144. Today, governing bodies throughout the world take enormous trouble to guard the welfare of the feline population; the British Governing Council has its Cat Care Committee, and in the USA the governing bodies have cat care high on their lists of priorities. The Cat Fanciers' Association, founded in 1906, has as one of its objects 'The promotion of the welfare of *all cats'.*[10]

The shorthair cats of the west were prominent in the growing Cat Fancy. Among the first to be exhibited at the newly-organised cat shows, they were the cared-for pets of people of leisure who could devote themselves to what was becoming a fascinating hobby. With the new understanding of hygiene, the huge advances in medical and veterinary knowledge, and the growth in popularity of the cat, the new century saw the dawn of a golden age for felines—not least for the once 'common-or-garden' shorthair, whose most attractive individuals were now being cherished to become the parents of the show cats in the growing fancy.

The Cat Club in England was founded by Lady Marcus Beresford, and the Beresford Cat Club in Chicago was named after her: some of its members founded the American Cat Association, the oldest governing body in the USA (Chapter 2). Those who fostered the cats formed societies to deal with all that concerned them, drew up registers to record their pedigrees, obtained for them all that could conduce to their welfare and their beauty, and lavished affection upon them. To see the cats of today is to realise how well they have profited by the good life that the twentieth century has brought them.

2

Standards and Varieties: I

The affairs of the Cat Fancy are dealt with by committees, as is the case with so many human activities. Governing bodies, founded when interest in cats was first becoming evident, have their sub-committees, for finance, discipline or other facets of their work; most important of all, such bodies keep the foundation records in which the pedigrees of the cats registered with them can be traced to their inception. Clubs and societies inaugurated for the breeding, fostering and exhibition of cats will be affiliated to a governing body, bound by its rules, and registering their kittens in its records.

Whenever breed societies have been started, dealing with particular cats, one of their first activities has been to draw up a standard of points for the exhibition qualities of the cats concerned; a club's committee will discuss and consider the cats, put its ideas before a general meeting of its members, hammer out an agreed standard, and send it to its governing body for approval. The case for the standard will be presented by the club's delegate to the governing body, and it will, possibly with some amendment, eventually be accepted as a provisional standard, later to be confirmed.

Such standards of points are the result of the deliberations of people who have carefully studied the cats, and they embody the preferences of the committees which draw them up. They are arbitrary, but a great deal of thought is given to them, and it can be said that they state the best features of the cats that they describe. With the passage of time, alterations may be made in a standard, again after discussion by the committees of clubs and their governing bodies. Such standards are of great importance in the feline world; breeders are concerned to produce kittens that will conform to them; judges will make awards according to them; the exhibits that best measure up to them will be the winning cats—the cats with the top prizes and the big rosettes, the ones whose progeny prospective purchasers will want to buy. These things are the measure of the importance of the standards, and the committees which drew them up certainly worked very hard.

Adherence to the accepted standards has, of course, tended to produce cats of an appearance more stereotyped than would have been found in nature without man's intervention (Chapter 5). To aim at producing and maintaining certain features will lead to a definite type, easily distinguished as a show cat rather than a common-or-garden moggie. Of all the varieties of cat carefully bred and perfected over the years, the domestic shorthair is the one who has best kept his natural features. Alterations there have been: puss-on-the-side-walk years ago had a very slightly pointed muzzle, less evident in the round face of his 'show' counterpart. But there has been less change in the appearance of this breed than in that of most exhibition cats. The standards to which they have been bred ask only for a perfecting of existing features.

The principal governing bodies give, in their standard of points booklets, a general standard which applies to all domestic shorthairs. The official general standard of the Governing Council of the Cat Fancy in Britain—used also in Australia and New Zealand—is headed:

British shorthairs

The British cat is compact, well-balanced and powerful, showing good depth of body, a full broad chest, short strong legs, rounded paws, tail thick at base with a rounded tip. The head is round with good width between the ears, round cheeks, firm chin, small ears, large round and well-opened eyes, with a short straight nose. The coat is short and dense.

Scale of points

Head	20
Eyes	10
Body	20
Legs and paws	10
Tail	10
Coat, colour and condition	30
	100

Head: Round and massive, with good breadth of skull. Round face with round underlying bone structure, well set on a short thick neck.

Nose: Short, broad and straight.

Chin: Firm and well developed.

Ears: Small, rounded at tips, with good width between and well furnished.

Eyes: Large, round, well opened, set wide apart and level.

Body: Well knit and powerful. Level back and deep broad chest.

Legs: Short, well boned and strong. Straight forelegs.

Paws: Round and firm.

Tail: Short and thick but in proportion to body length with a rounded tip.

Coat: Short and dense.

Condition: Hard and muscular.

Faults: Tail defects, definite nose-stops. Overlong or fluffy coat.

The American Cat Association, the oldest governing body in the United States, gives the following:

Basic domestic shorthair standard

Scale of points. To be applied to domestic shorthairs

Head	10
Ears	5
Eyes (total deduct for wrong colour)	10
Body form	15
Legs and feet	10
Tail	5
Colour and markings	25
Coat and condition	20
	100

Only cats scoring 85 or more points in a recognised breed are eligible for winners.

Head: 10 points

Broad, with cheeks well-developed, especially in studs. Nose and face medium short with eyes set wide apart. Muzzle should be squarish in appearance, but should not be foreshortened or peke-faced. Chin well-developed, forming a perpendicular line with upper lip.

Undesirable: long nose or wedge-shaped head; weak, receding chin.

Ears: 5 points
Medium in size and set forward and pricked, rounded at tips and not too large at base. Undesirable: long pointed ears, set wide, or ears set too close together.

Eyes: 10 points
Eye opening should be oval, set to show breadth of nose. Eye colour must conform to requirements listed in Persian cat; except where orange or copper eye is called for, eye colour shall be gold.
Undesirable: narrow or round eyes.

Body form: 15 points
The domestic shorthair ranges in size from medium to large. Females should be slightly smaller than males, but should not be frail or dainty in appearance. The body should be well-knit, heavily-built, powerful, showing good depth and a full chest. Neck medium short and denoting strength, but in proportion to the body.
Undesirable: too foreshortened and stocky or too long, sleek or oriental in appearance; neck too short and thick, too long and slender.

Legs and feet: 10 points
Legs should be of good substance and in proportion to the body. Feet well rounded. Five toes in front, four in back. *Withhold winners for extra toes.*

Tail: 5 points
Tail length should be in proportion to the body, thick at the base and tapering gradually to a blunt end. Tail should be carried almost level with back.
Undesirable: thin, whip-like tail, too thick, too short or carried over back.

Colour and markings: 25 points
Coat colour shall be as described in Persian colour standards. Allowance to be made for faint Tabby markings on tail and legs in kittens and young cats. For cats with special markings, the 25 points allowed for colour to be divided 15 points for markings and 10 for colour. In Tortoiseshell and Blue-Cream, a slight amount of brindling may not be penalised.

Coat and condition: 20 points

Coat shall be short and close-lying. It should also be lustrous, thick (but not double) and even-textured. Cat should be hard and muscular giving a general appearance of power and activity. Neat and clean. All physical aspects of the cat should complement each other to present a perfect picture. Temperamentally gentle and amenable to handling. Undesirable: fine, thin coat or long, fluffy-textured coat. Allowance to be made for lack of closeness or lustre in Blues.

This is an extremely detailed preamble, and it is almost the only American standard not in complete accord with the British: the ACA standard asks for an oval eye-opening, and states unequivocally that round eyes are undesirable, whereas the British standard asks that the eyes of these cats be 'large, round and well-opened.' Widely-separated populations of any species may, of course, develop differences in course of time, but oddly enough, the Cat Fanciers' Association standard asks for a round eye, as do those of the Cat Fanciers' Federation and the Crown Cat Fanciers' Federation, all important USA governing bodies.

The ACA directive differs from the British on two other counts: under it, ears must be 'medium in size, set forward and pricked', which gives a picture contrary to the British 'small, rounded at tips.' As to the other point on which these two standards differ, the ACA standard has 'Allowance to be made for lack of closeness or lustre in Blues', whereas European, and indeed other American standards make no distinction between the quality of coats of different colours.

The ACA directive makes the point that polydactyly shall be penalised, and stresses that the tail shall not be carried over the back. This last is not a common fault, but it certainly looks strange when it occurs; there is a Siamese neutered pet who carries his tail as would a Pekinese dog, and the effect is to make people laugh! Under *Coat and Condition* the ACA standard has 'neat and clean...temperamentally gentle and amenable to handling.' This lends emphasis to the oft-given advice to exhibitors: present your exhibit perfectly-groomed, and if you are unlucky enough to own a cat who has winning qualities but a nervous disposition—don't show him (Chapter 8).

The Cat Fancier's Association, the biggest governing body in the

United States, has a long and detailed introduction to its official standards for American shorthairs.

American shorthairs

Point score

Head (including size and shape of eyes, ear-shape and set)	30
Type (including shape, size, bone and length of tail)	20
Coat	10
Condition	10
Colour	20
Eye colour	10
	100

General The American shorthair...has for many, many centuries adapted itself willingly and cheerfully to the needs of man, but without allowing itself to become effete or its natural intelligence to diminish. Its disposition and habits are exemplary as a household pet, a pet and companion for children, but the feral instinct lies not far beneath the surface and this breed of cat remains capable of self-sufficiency when the need arises. Its hunting instinct is so strong that it exercises the skill even when well provided with food. This is our only breed of true 'working cat'. The conformation of the breed is well adapted for this and reflects its refusal to surrender its natural functions. This is a cat lithe enough to stalk its prey, but powerful enough to make the kill easily. Its reflexes are under perfect control. Its legs are long enough to cope with any terrain and heavy and muscular enough for high leaps. The face is long enough to permit easy grasping by the teeth with jaws so powerful that they can close against resistance. Its coat is dense enough to protect from moisture, cold and superficial skin injuries, but short enough and of sufficiently hard texture to resist matting or entanglement when slipping through heavy vegetation. No part of the anatomy is so exaggerated as to foster weakness. The general effect is that of the trained athlete with all muscles rippling easily beneath the skin, the flesh lean and hard, and with great latent power held in reserve.

Head: Large, with full-cheeked face giving the impression of an oblong just slightly longer than wide.

Neck: Medium in length, muscular and strong.

Nose: Medium in length, same width for entire length, with a gentle curve.

Muzzle: Squared, definite jowls in studs.

Chin: Firm and well-developed, forming perpendicular line with upper lip.

Ears: Medium, slightly rounded at tips, wide and not unduly open at base.

Eyes: Round and wide with slight slant to outer aperture. Set well apart. Bright, clear and alert.

Body: Medium to large, well knit, powerful and hard with well-developed chest and heavy shoulders. No sacrifice of quality for the sake of mere size.

Legs: Medium in length, firm-boned and heavily muscled, showing capability for easy jumping.

Paws: Firm, full and rounded, with heavy pads. Toes five in front, four behind.

Tail: Medium long, heavy at base, tapering to an abrupt blunt end in appearance, but with normal tapering final vertebrae.

Coat: Short, thick, even and hard in texture. Somewhat heavier and thicker during the winter months.

Condition: Springy in movement, with muscles lithe and rippling. framework well padded with hard, lean flesh, giving the general effect of tremendous energy and power held in reserve.

Penalize: Excessive cobbiness or ranginess. Very short tail. obesity or boniness.

Withhold winners: Kinked or abnormal tail. Locket or button. Deep nose break. Long or fluffy fur. Any appearance of hybridisation with any other breed. Incorrect number of toes.

There can surely be no more carefully detailed standard than this; it leaves no excuse for exhibitors or judges at CFA shows not to know the features required by their governing body. The statement that the domestic shorthair's 'hunting instinct is so strong that it exercises the skill even when well-provided with food' may perhaps be amplified: it is the well-fed cat who makes the good hunter—a starved cat will not have the strength and energy needed to deal with his prey (Chapter 1). It is of course perfectly true that the cat has for many, many centuries adapted itself willingly and cheerfully to the needs of man. The cat is the cleverest of the domestic animals. Man did not choose him, as he chose sheep and cattle—the cat chose man. *Felis domesticus* undoubtedly found warmth by man's earliest fires, shelter in his caves and pickings in his rubbish dumps. This suited primitive man very well, for the cat slaughtered the rodents who were also interested in the rubbish. So the exquisitely clean, quiet cat edged his clever way into the comfort and safety provided by another species.

Certainly the domestic cat keeps his independence; his pact with man is of mutual advantage: he gives man his loveliness, his skill in destroying vermin, his charming, purring ways; and man provides him with good living and with all the benefits of scientific advance; his continuance in man's homes reflects his appreciation of safety and shelter, his purring shows his pleasure in warmth and in the grooming that man's stroking hands gives. Nevertheless he retains his independence, coming to man's call if he is hungry, but not if he is sleepy or busy with a mouse or a vole.

As is often the case in American show standards, CFA has a splendid description of the domestic shorthair's chin as it should be: firm and well developed, forming a perpendicular line with the upper lip. This brings to mind at once the admirable profile of the shorthair at his best.

Tabbies

The various governing bodies have approved show standards for colour and pattern in the different breeds of shorthairs, and of them all, the Tabby has a special importance: he is perhaps the earliest of our felines, and his coat pattern is the basis for many of the charming 'new' show varieties of today; the Silver Tabby, perhaps, in particular, since from his lovely patterning are derived the new and intriguing Tipped cat and also Shaded Silver and Smoke shorthairs as well as the Chinchillas and the Shaded Silver and Smoke longhairs.

The American Cat Association's show standard reads:

Classic Tabby pattern

To conform with the standard and be eligible for winners, the Tabby cat must show good contrast between the ground colour and the deep heavy markings. Head barred, with frown marks extending between the ears and down to the shoulders, which divides the head lines from the spine. Butterfly on shoulders. These back markings or spinals consist of a distinct wide dark centre stripe with stripes of the ground colour on either side and these in turn bordered by a second dark stripe. The dark swirls on the cheeks and side of the body shall make complete unbroken circles and shall be centred by a large dark spot surrounded by the ground colour. Legs are evenly barred with the bracelets coming to meet the body markings. Tail evenly barred.

Mackerel Tabby

Marking dense, clearly defined, and all narrow pencillings. Legs evenly barred with narrow bracelets coming up to meet the body markings. Tail barred. Necklaces on neck and chest distinct, like so many chains. Head barred with an 'M' on the forehead. Unbroken lines running back from the eyes. Lines running down the head to meet the shoulders. Spine lines run together to form a narrow saddle. Narrow pencilling runs around the body.

The Cat Fanciers' Association standards give:

Classic Tabby pattern

Markings dense, clearly defined and broad. Legs evenly barred with bracelets coming up to meet the body markings. Tail evenly ringed. Several unbroken necklaces on neck and upper chest, the more the better. Frown marks on forehead form intricate letter 'M'. Unbroken lines run back from outer corner of eye. Swirls on cheeks. Vertical lines over back of head extend to shoulder markings which are in the shape of a butterfly with both upper and lower wings clearly outlined and marked with dots inside outline. Back markings consist of a vertical line down the spine from butterfly to tail with a vertical stripe parallelling it on each side, the three stripes well separated by stripes of the ground colour. Large solid blotch on each side to be encircled by one or more unbroken rings. Side markings should be the same on both sides. Double vertical row of buttons on chest and stomach.

Mackerel Tabby pattern

Markings dense, clearly defined and all narrow pencillings. Legs evenly barred with narrow bracelets coming up to meet the body markings. Tail barred. Necklaces on neck and chest, like so many chains. Head barred with an 'M' on the forehead. Unbroken lines running back from the eyes. Lines running down the head to meet the shoulders. Spine lines run together to form a narrow saddle. Narrow pencillings run around body. Lips and chin the same shade as the rings around the eyes.

In Britain, The Governing Council's standard runs:

Classic Tabby pattern
All markings to be clearly defined and dense. Legs barred evenly with bracelets going down from the body markings to the toes. Ground colour and markings should be equally balanced. Evenly ringed tail. On the neck and upper chest there should be unbroken necklaces, the more the better. On the forehead there should be a letter 'M' made by frown marks. There should be an unbroken line running back from the outer corner of the eye. There should be pencillings on the cheeks. There should be a vertical line which runs over the back of the head and extends to the shoulder markings, which should be shaped like a butterfly. Both the upper and the lower wings should be defined clearly in outline with dots inside this outline. On the back there should be a line running down the spine from the butterfly to the tail, and there should be a stripe on each side of this running parallel to it. These stripes should be separated from each other by stripes of the ground colour. On each flank there should be a large solid oyster or blotch which should be surrounded by one or more unbroken rings. The markings on each side should be identical. All Tabby cats should be spotted in the abdominal region. In all Tabby cats the tails should be evenly ringed.

Mackerel Tabby pattern
Head, legs and tail as for Classic Tabby. There should be a narrow unbroken line running from the back of the head to the base of the tail. The rest of the body to be covered with narrow lines running vertically down from the spine line and to be unbroken. These lines should be as narrow and as numerous as possible.

Pattern faults: Solid back, broken tail rings. Solid sides, white tip to tail and white anywhere. Spotting on back. Brindling.

Withhold certificates: Incorrect eye-colour. White anywhere. Incorrect mackerel pattern.

It should, perhaps, be mentioned that the 'frown lines' are not the result of any wrinkling of the forehead by the cat, but are part of the pattern. It is noteworthy that these standards conform: their wording is by no means identical, but their requirements are the same; the descriptions given by the various governing bodies do not contradict each other.

Students of Tabby patterning in the domestic cat have always described its manifestations as 'Blotched, Striped and Spotted.' And the fancy's standards given above for Classic Tabby and Mackerel Tabby are good descriptions of the 'blotched' and 'striped' cats.

Spotted Tabbies (USA: Ticked Tabbies)

In Britain, Spotted Tabbies were first recognised and granted championship status as pedigree varieties comparatively recently: I can remember a show not so very many years ago at which Mr Will Lamb, afterwards Treasurer to the Council, who had made a study of them, showed me and a colleague what points to look for in a small class of these cats. However, this was not the first appearance of Spotted cats at a championship show in England; the list of classes given in the Gordon Stables book of the 1870s includes 'Class VII is for Spotted Tabby'; and the author describes the cat as follows: 'A broad black band ran along his back and down his fine tail; and diverging from this band came dark stripes of colour down the sides, converging round the thighs, and swirling round his chest in two Lord Mayor's chains; but the stripes had this peculiarity, they were all *broken up into spots*'.[1]

Here is the Governing Council standard for the Spotted Tabby:

Head markings: As Classic Tabby.
Body and legs: Good, clear spotting essential. Spots as numerous and distinct as possible.
Tail: Spots or broken rings desirable.
Colour: Silver with black spots. Brown with black spots. Red with deep red spots. Any other recognised ground colours acceptable with appropriate spotting.
Eye colour: Silver Spotted, green or hazel. Brown Spotted, orange, hazel or deep yellow. Red Spotted, brilliant copper.
Nose leather and paws: As for Classic Tabby.
Faults: Solid spine.
Pattern faults: (e.g. linked spots). Brindling. White tip to tail. White anywhere.
Withhold certificates: Incorrect eye-colour. Incorrect pattern. White anywhere.

In the USA, the Crown Cat Fanciers' Association, which names the Spotteds 'Ticked Tabbies', gives:

Ticked Tabby pattern: (Shorthair). Ticked Tabby differs from the mackerel in that all markings except head, bracelets, necklaces and tail rings are composed of a series of dots. Ideally marked Ticked Tabbies have an equal amount of ground colour between dots. Dots vary from true circle to half-moons... True circle is ideal.

Objections: Solid spine lines.

Faults: Solid mackerel markings and dots that meld together.

The Cat Fanciers' Federation describes the Ticked Tabby thus:
The Ticked Tabby differs from the Mackerel Tabby in that all markings except head, bracelets, necklaces and tail rings are composed of a series of dots. Ideally marked Tabbies (ticked) have an equal amount of ground colour between dots. Dots vary from true circles to half-moons, true circles being the ideal. Spine lines are often solid but should be dotted. Objections: solid mackerel markings or dots that meld together.

Many of these cats have very clear, distinct spots, and these may be not only circular or half-moon shaped as described by CFF and CFA but sometimes pyramidal. Such markings on the flanks of a really good Spotted Tabby make an arrestingly effective pattern. One of the most beautiful ever to be exhibited in England was Brynbuboo Bosselot, bred by Mrs Absalom. He was sweet-tempered, a lovely example of his variety—a beautiful Brown Spotted Tabby.

Brown Tabbies

Colouring for the Brown Tabbies is described by the Governing Council standard of points as brilliant coppery brown ground with dense black markings. Back of legs from paw to heel should be black. Eye colour, orange, hazel or deep yellow. Nose leather, brick red. Pads black or brown. Faults: brindling.

The Cat Fanciers' Association asks for:

Colour: Ground colour brilliant coppery brown, markings dense black. Lips and chin the same shade as the rings around the eyes. Back of leg black from paws to heel. Nose leather: Brick red. Paw pads: Black or brown. Eye colour: Brilliant gold.

The American Cat Association's instructions are:

Brown Tabby: Ground colour including lips and chin a rich tawny brown. Markings dense black and clearly defined. Eyes: copper. Undesirable: Grey undercoat or ground colour, pale or indistinct markings.

The Brown Tabbies have a peculiar attrraction, for they are the cared-for, perfected descendants of some of the oldest cats known in the world. A Thai lady once said 'The ordinary cat in Bangkok is the common-or-garden Tabby'[2]; and English folk in town and country have for centuries thought of the little cat in city or village as patterned in black and brown: a sturdy, healthy, self-sufficient Tabby cat. The Reverend Mr Rees, for many years Vice-Chairman of the Governing Council in earlier days, loved the Brown Tabbies, and bred them and cared for them as their beauty grew towards its present perfection.

Silver Tabbies

Some of the Tabbies of long ago had more grey than brown in their coats, and from these the cat fancy has bred one of our most lovely shorthairs: the Silver Tabby.

For colour in this variety, the Cat Fanciers' Association demands:
Silver Tabby: Pale, clear silver. Markings dense black.
Nose leather: Brick red.
Paw pads: Black.
Eye colour: Green or hazel.

The American Cat Association:
Silver Tabby: Must be a pure pale silver with decided jet black markings. Eyes, blue-green. Undesirable: dark or white spots, muddy colour without clear differentiation.

The Governing Council standard:
Silver Tabby: Clear silver ground colour which should include chin and legs. Markings dense black. Eye colour green or hazel. Nose leather brick red for preference, although black is permissible. Pads black. Soles of feet from toes to heels black.
Faults: Brown on nose or paws. Brindling.
Withhold certificates: Incorrect eye-colour. White anywhere. Incorrect Tabby pattern.

These cats are some of the most beautiful to be seen at the championship shows of today: they have been bred with a lovely silver ground for their dark markings, and the black patterning on silver, and with no white, is unusual and attractive. From them are derived some of our most spectacular cats: notably, from the long-hair Silver Tabbies come those exquisite creatures the Chinchillas, whose coats are like gauze and silver; but also, more recently,

Smokes, Shaded Silvers and the Tipped Shorthairs.

Red Tabbies
There are also the Red Tabbies, those magnificent cats with bright, orange coats who have evolved from the old-fashioned 'ginger' cats, and governing bodies have drawn up standards of points for their coat-colour as follows.

The Cat Fanciers' Association has:

Red Tabby: Ground colour red. Markings deep rich red. Lips and chin red.

Nose leather: Brick red.

Paw pads: Brick red.

Eye colour: Brilliant gold.

The Governing Council's standard reads: red ground colour and markings of deep rich red. Eye colour, brilliant copper. Nose leather, brick red. Pads, deep red. Sides of feet, dark red.

The Cat Fanciers' Federation gives: ground colour red, with dense darker red markings. Leather, pink. Eyes, brilliant orange or deep copper.

As descriptions of beautiful creatures and as clear directives for exhibitors and judges, the Tabby standards really leave nothing to be desired.

3

Standards and Varieties: II

The Red, Cream and Tortoiseshell shorthairs are the 'coloured cats' of the English countryside, the prettily patch-coated cats prized by cottagers since Europe's Middle Ages.

Reds

It has for centuries been said that 'a ginger cat is always a Tom', but this is not in fact true; because of the unusual behaviour of the gene for red in feline coat-colour, more red males are born than red females: the females tend to be Tortoiseshells (Chapter 1). But when two cats, both with red in their coats, are mated, red females as well as red males will appear in the resulting litter.

It is not often that a cat with a self-red coat is seen. I once found two, playing together in a village garden; I could not discover any patterning whatever on them; but, as a rule, the exhibition Reds at championship shows are Red Tabbies. Yet the important governing bodies give standards of points for Self-Red cats. The Governing Council has a standard for Self-Red longhairs, but none for their shorthair counterparts; the American Cat Association lays down that standards for shorthair colour and markings in these cats shall be as under its Persian colour standards, and gives its longhair colour standard in the solid colour division:

Red: Uniform deep, rich, clear red throughout, without ticking, Tabby markings or shading...Eyes copper.

The very important Cat Fanciers' Association, however, gives under American shorthair colours:

Red: deep, rich, clear, brilliant red; without shading, markings or ticking. Lips and chin the same colour as coat.

Nose leather: Brick red.

Paw Pads: Brick red.

Eye colour: Brilliant gold.

Thus it is clear that governing bodies worldwide accept Self-Red as a separate variety. Very, very seldom, however, is such a cat seen; the protective pattern, hiding the primeval cat from his predators by merging him with his surroundings, and forming part of the threat display with which he warns his enemies, is very slow to be lost from the coat of *Felis domesticus*. It even sometimes appears, plain to be seen, upon the near-white thighs and flanks of Siamese cats.

Tortoiseshells

The Governing Council standard for the Tortoiseshells, who are the dams of the Reds and Creams, has:

Colour: Black, with brilliant patches of cream and red. All these patches should be clearly defined and well broken on the legs and body. A red or cream blaze on the head is desirable. Nose leather pink and/or black. Eyes brilliant copper or orange.

Faults: Tabby markings. Brindling. White anywhere. Colour unbroken on paws. Unequal balance of colour.

Withhold certificates: Incorrect eye colour. White anywhere. Green rims.

Under American shorthair colours, the Cat Fanciers' Association has:

Colour: Black with unbrindled patches of red and cream. Patches clearly defined and unbroken on both body and extremities. Blaze of red or cream on face is desirable.

Eye colour: Brilliant gold.

The American Cat Association directs that colour shall be as described in Persian standards and gives:

Colour: The three colours, black, orange (red) and cream—shall be well broken over entire body with colours bright and well defined and free from tabby markings. 'Blaze' (half of forehead, nose and chin and lips black and half orange (red) alternating preferred).

Legs: Blocked but not barred and feet showing similar pattern to face, i.e. toes differing in colour.

Eyes: Copper.

Undesirable: Brindled colours rather than blocked, tabby markings or stripes or bars, solid colour on face, legs or tail.

The ACA directive for 'toes differing in colour' brings to mind the charming effect of the differently-coloured toes upon the paw-pads:

1 Timothy. Brown Tabby owned by Sam L. Scheer of Colorado.
(Photo: Sam L. Scheer)

2 *Right* Little Pink Panters Joris. Brown Tabby owned by B. de Graaf. (By courtesy of Hetty van Winsen)

3 *Below* Brown Tabby owned by Mrs Absalom. (Photo: Anne Cumbers)

4 Silver Tabby owned by Mrs B. Eleved. (By courtesy of Hetty van Winsen)

5 Silver Tabby owned by Mrs Haymes. (Photo: Anne Cumbers)

6 Red Tabby kitten, five months. (Photo: Anne Cumbers)

7 Red Tabby Killinghall Red Phantasy at five months. Bred by Miss Hardman, owned by Mrs Hamilton. (Photo: Jane Hamilton)

in a Tortoiseshell, the pads will vary with the fur on the toes, a cream-furred toe having a pale pink pad, a black-furred toe a black pad, and so on. This Association adds to its colour directive: 'Colour and markings make the class and *must* conform.' This is reminiscent of the teaching of an eminent British judge of years ago, the late B. A. Stirling-Webb, who told newly-appointed judges: 'When you judge a cat, begin by making sure that he is what he purports to be.'

The best of the Tortoiseshells show in their coats the three colours — black, red, and the cream that is the dilute of red.

Creams

The tabby striations of the old protective marking are as often present in the shorthair Creams as in any other feline coat, and the British standard makes some allowance for this:

Colour: Lighter shades preferred. Level in colour and free from markings. No sign of white anywhere.

Eyes: Copper or orange.

Nose leather and pads: Pink.

Withhold certificates: Incorrect eye colour. Green rims. Heavy tabby markings.

In the United States, however, a distinction is made between a Cream and a Cream Tabby. Thus the Cat Fanciers' Association, in its list of American shorthair colours, has:

Cream: One level shade of buff cream, without markings. Sound to the roots. Lighter shades preferred. *Nose leather:* Pink. *Paw pads:* Pink. *Eye colour:* Brilliant gold.

And also gives:

Cream Tabby: Ground colour very pale cream. Markings of buff and cream sufficiently darker than the ground colour to afford good contrast but remaining within the dilute colour range. *Nose leather:* Pink. *Paw pads:* Pink. *Eye colour:* Brilliant gold.

The American Cat Association has:

Cream: Uniform shade of cream, neither beige nor light red nor orange. *Eyes*: copper. Full 10 points deducted for green eyes. *Undesirable*: shading, light spots and tabby markings.

Cream Tabby: The ground colour should be cream with dense, darker cream markings. *Eyes should be copper.*

Clearly, the question of patterning presents a problem; indeed, it is possible for big kittens and even very young adults to have uniformly cream coats, and yet for distinct striations to become evident before they are two years old; so that sometimes, in the USA, an alteration in registration may be necessary. The shade of colour, too, must vary: between the darkest red and palest cream there is a very wide range of shades.

Blue-Creams

The charming Blue-Creams of our show standards are, in fact, Tortoiseshells: they are the dilute manifestation of the Torties, blue being a dilution of melanin (black), and cream of red. A really well mingled Blue-Cream coat is extremely beautiful; the cats have, of course, the sturdy shorthair type, and the colour standards for them are as follows:

Governing Council:

Colour: Blue and cream to be softly intermingled. No blaze.

Eyes: Copper or orange.

Nose leather: Blue.

Pads: Blue and/or Pink.

Faults: Tabby markings. White anywhere. Colour unbroken on paws. Unequal balance of colour.

Withhold certificate: Incorrect eye colour. Green rims. Solid patches of colour.

The Cat Fanciers' Association:

Colour: Blue with patches of solid cream. Patches clearly defined and well broken on both body and extremities.

Eye colour: Brilliant gold.

The American Cat Association:

Colour: The two colours, blue and cream, shall be arranged to conform to the Tortoiseshell standard.

Eyes: Copper.

The Crown Cat Fanciers' Federation:

Colour: The two colours, clear blue and cream, should be evenly divided and broken into patches that are bright and well defined. Face should have characteristic blaze.

Eyes: Brilliant copper or deep orange.

This is a rare instance of a pronounced difference between the USA and UK standards for any variety of cat. Beauty, of course, 'is in the eye of the beholder'. Some of the Tortoiseshell kittens born had in their coats brilliant patches of colour, in others, the colours were intermingled. As always, committee decisions were made; oddly, in Britain it was decided to aim for a clearly-patched coat and blaze in the red/black Tortoiseshells, and for softly intermingled colours and no blaze in the Blue-Creams. In America, the blaze and the clear patching were admired in all Tortoiseshells, Blue-Creams included.

Some years ago, in a Berkshire cottage garden, there were two Blue-Cream kittens, born to a little grey-coated cat whose mate had been the local Tom—a very pale 'ginger'. The kittens had no known ancestry at all. Their type was good, as often happens in the strong, natural shorthairs, for the fancy has adhered in its standards to the firm type, and very frequently the cat on the sidewalk has conformation fit for the show pen. These kittens could not successfully have been exhibited in Britain, even if they had been registered, for each had a cream blaze, and each had even patches of bright colour, well-defined. If they had had known ancestry and could have been exhibited in the USA, they would have been worthy contenders!

There are many tales told of the Tortoiseshells, some of them apocryphal. Perhaps the least credible are those which relate behaviour to coat-colour. Gordon Stables, in his book of over a century ago, firmly attributes different characters to felines of differing coat colours. In his list of classes at the Birmingham and Crystal Palace shows he describes the exhibits entered in them, and his description of the Red Tabby in class V includes: 'The Red Tabby ought to approach in size and shape, nearly to the Brown. They are the same kind-hearted, good-natured animals as their brown brethren, and as a rule are better hunters. They go farther afield and tackle larger game... .They are often, moreover, very expert fishers.' This makes a comparison between the qualities of differently coloured cats, and claims positive differences in behaviour as being connected with colour.

This author of a hundred years ago, who calls the exhibitions of his day 'Pussy shows', and writes of the Brown Tabbies that they 'possess all pussy's noblest attributes to perfection! They are docile, honest and faithful...', says of the judging of Reds 'Urbanity of countenance not to be overlooked'; and of the Brown Tabbies that they 'seldom take undue advantage of their great strength.' Such pronouncements, seriously connecting behaviour and character with coat-colour, can only seem comical to late twentieth century minds. Yet....some years ago I bred a nice Tortoiseshell kitten who, in fact, won her open class at the Southern Cat Club's Show in London, and an older colleague asked me 'Does she play with water?' I admitted with surprise that this kitten dearly loved a tap left dripping and would sit hitting droplets of water with her paws. 'Tortoiseshells always do,' said my friend quite seriously, and I realised with surprise that of the many kittens I had bred this, the only Tortoiseshell, was also the only one who played with water.

As to 'urbanity of countenance', it should be noted that some modern standards have asked for 'a pleasing expression.' It is, incidentally, interesting that the Peke-faced Persian, bred only in the USA, is a red-coated cat; the Cat Fanciers' Federation in its standard for these cats, states 'The Peke-faced Persian is recognised in the solid Red and Red Tabby colours... . The eyes...have a different expression from the regular standard Persian.'

This is, in fact, perfectly reasonable: these cats get their name from the Pekinese dogs that they resemble, and a feature of their appearance is that they have, like the little dogs, prominent eyes; this, plainly, is enough to give the impression of a different expression and, in fact, these longhairs are often called 'owl-eyed'. There is, of course, no shorthair equivalent for them.

The Stables comparison of angling ability in cats of different colours is curious; cats are not usually very successful 'fishers'; for though they are fond of fish, and have occasionally been known to catch and eat one, their efforts as anglers generally result in the death of the prey from a blow dealt by the cat's claws, but without the cat being able to catch the fish.

In breeding these cats for show, it is important to remember that their eyes must be yellow, and preferably its deeper shades, copper or orange, and that cream coats must be pale, and red coats deeply 'ginger'. It is worth remembering that more and deeper gold will appear in the coats of Tortoiseshell and Red kittens as they grow older.

Blues

The Blue domestic shorthair of the show pen is the highly-bred descendant of the grey 'cat on the sidewalk'. It is true that there is, in fact, blue in the coats of these cats, as evidenced by photographs taken in certain lights, in which the subject appears more blue than any cat ever looked to human eye; further, the sun's actinic rays will bring out the blue in the cat's fur.

There are other blue shorthairs besides the British/American cat who comes under the heading Blue domestic shorthair[1]; Burmese, once always brown cats, are now bred in other colours, and Blue Burmese are attractive cats: they are recognised in Britain, Australia and New Zealand, and by some, but not all, of the governing bodies in the USA; in America, where the Burmese was first established by Dr Thompson as a show cat, there is a strong body of opinion that 'a Burmese cat is a sable cat'; however, the Cat Fanciers' Federation, for one, has a standard for Blue Burmese. Another blue shorthair is the Korat, also first established in the USA, by Mrs Daphne Negus; this little cat, with his heart-shaped face, has always been a blue cat. Finally, the Russian Blue, at present (1980) making a 'come-back' in England and, particularly, in Australia, is, as his name indicates, a blue cat.

These three varieties are all of foreign type, and their provenance is Eastern; they are listed as foreign shorthairs, as opposed to American or British shorthairs, in standards and in schedules and catalogues on both sides of the Atlantic. But their appearance at exhibitions has caused, now and then, the comment 'Oh—just another blue cat!' This is not quite fair, since although the colour is the same, yet not only the type of the cats but the quality of their coat also, is distinctly unlike in the different varieties: Russian Blues of quality have been rare, since for some reason they have not been carefully bred since the early 1950s; but breeders are now, since the 1970s, concentrating upon their show qualities, and some have appeared, particularly in Australia, with coats that are, as their standard demands, '...standing up soft and silky.' It is the 'standing up' manifestation that is unmistakable and not like any other blue coat. The fur of the Korat is silver-blue, each hair being tipped with silver, producing an effect that is unique to this cat; and the Blue Burmese has fur of the same kind as is found in all Burmese—short, fine, lying close to the body, feeling like satin to the touch. In each of these Foreign Blue varieties the fur is quite different, and all their coats differ not only from each other but from the Blue domestic shorthair, with his immensely thick, short fur.

The directive for the coats of British shorthairs is that they shall be 'short and dense', and in a good show cat, the fur is indeed so dense that it is difficult to find the skin; this coat is quite distinct from the pelage of any other cat. Here are the colour standards:

Governing Council:
Colours: Light to medium blue. Even colour and no Tabby markings or white anywhere.
Eyes: Copper or orange.
Nose leather and pads: Blue
Faults: Unsound coats. Silver tipping to coats.
Withhold certificates: Incorrect eye-colour. Green rims.

The Cat Fanciers' Association:
Blue: Blue, lighter shade preferred, one level tone from nose to tip of tail. Sound to the roots. A sound darker shade is more acceptable than an unsound lighter shade.

The American Cat Association:
British Blue standard
Colour: Light to medium blue, very even and without Tabby markings or shadings. *No white.*
Eyes: Orange, yellow or copper. Green tinge not allowed.

Again, there is here unanimity of thinking about these cats. It is noteworthy that ACA calls them British Blues and it may be that some of their ancestors were imported into the USA from Britain. The silver tipping mentioned as undesirable in the British standard suggests that the gene for silver could be involved. Tipping, so admired in the hairs of Russian Blues, Chinchillas and the recently-bred shorthair Tipped cats, is extremely rare in British Blues: in all my years of judging I have not seen one. In France, the Blue shorthairs are known as Chartreux. There has, now and then, been put forward the idea that the British Blues and the Chartreux were different varieties of shorthair cats; but well-known judges in France and Britain have always been aware that the two terms are simply different names for the same cat. The Blue shorthair doubtless existed in France and England in the Middle Ages; it is quite reasonable, indeed, to suppose that he voyaged as ship's cat from Calais to Dover and back and if the fancy took him, went ashore and settled in either country. After all, there were in mediaeval days no quarantine laws to prevent him!

The Cat Fanciers' Association stresses the importance of

evenness of colour: 'sound to the roots'. This Association makes the point that a dark coat of even colour is better than a pale coat whose colour is uneven. This is an important pronouncement. Major Dugdale, a British international judge of distinction, used to tell novices that of two cats of otherwise equal merit, they should choose the paler—but he would never have advised anybody to favour a coat that was not sound. You can, at shows today, see a judge part the fur of a Blue to make sure the hairs are of the same shade from root to tip. In appraising a longhair, it is possible to 'puff open' the coat, just blowing it lightly, so that the fur is visible down to the skin; with a shorthair, the coat can easily be parted with the fingers. The Blues are among the aristocrats of the feline world, and are extensively bred and exhibited; from the Chartreux of Paris and the French provinces to a lovely British Blue belonging to Mrs Lorna Thomas of Western Australia, this variety is admired.

Oddly, the Blue was not, apparently, shown a century ago; in the Gordon Stables book lists of the classes at cat shows held at the Crystal Palace and at Birmingham have no class for the Blue cat, although mention is made of 'Blue or Silver Tabby', and also, under 'Unusual Colour', a 'Maltese', all of one colour, 'a strange sort of slate colour or blue: even the whiskers were of the same hue...'.

Whites

The standards for the White shorthairs run as follows:

Governing Council:
White blue-eyed
Colour: White to be pure, untinged with yellow.
Eyes: Very deep sapphire blue. No green rims or flecks. Dark mark on head permissible in kittens. Nose leather pink. Pads pink.
Withhold certificates: Incorrect eye-colour. Green rims.

White odd-eyed
Colour: White to be pure, untinged with yellow.
Eyes: One gold, orange or copper. One blue. No green rims or flecks.
Nose leather and pads: Pink.

The Cat Fanciers' Assocation asks for:
White: Pure glistening white.
Nose leather: Pink.
Paw pads: Pink.

Eye colour: Deep blue or brilliant gold. Odd-eyed Whites shall have one blue and one copper eye with equal colour depth.

The American Cat Association:
White: Pure white, no coloured hairs.
Eyes: Blue, copper blue, and copper. Deeper shades preferred. Full 10 points deducted for green eyes.

Again, these standards show like thinking, and the Cat Fanciers' Association's 'Pure glistening white' describes perfectly the white coat at its best.

It is curious that white cats can be odd-eyed, and there is at present (1980) no satisfactory explanation for this, which may be due to some genetic factor not yet isolated. M. N. Batten states: 'It has been postulated that the reason for the blue eye is the presence of the factor S'.[1] 'S' means white spotting, and this is a factor that will produce in the cat blue eye-colour, and deafness in one or both ears, the deafness coinciding with the blue eyes. It seems however, that a cat may have blue eyes without 'S' being present. In the White cat since he is white all over, it is not possible to recognise the presence of white spotting unless the effects of this character are present: if a white cat has a blue eye and is deaf on the same side—or both eyes blue and complete deafness—then the presence of 'S' can be inferred, with patches of white spotting over one or both eyes. Although it is not at present known why these cats can be odd-eyed, we do know what can be expected from different matings. The genetics of eye-colour have always been difficult, in man as well as in the cat, but blue eye-colour is a simple recessive to orange; thus blue-eyed cat mated to blue-eyed cat will produce only blue-eyed kittens. But from matings between two orange-eyed cats, or between an orange-eyed cat and an odd-eyed cat, orange, blue, and odd-eyed kittens may appear.

'Some odd-eyed Whites have one orange eye and one green eye'.[2] If an orange-eyed White be mated to a Chinchilla, the kittens will invariably have poor eye-colour, or one orange eye and one green. Breeders have sometimes favoured the cross-orange-eyed White Chinchilla because this results in a crystal purity of the coat, with no yellow tinge; but this is not often resorted to, and it is not to be wondered at. Mrs Batten writes that this mating is seldom carried out, for its effect on eye-colour is adverse, and breeders must be prepared to spend several generations of breeding back to orange-eyed Whites to regain the good eye-colour, by which time the purity of coat gained from the Chinchilla mating may be lost. The Chinchilla, with his lovely, fairy-tale, silvered coat, is of course a longhair: the shorthair Chinchilla is the 'new' variety known as the Tipped cat (Chapter 4).

Probably the most important show character of the Whites is the purity of the coat-colour, with not the faintest trace of yellow. In years gone by some lovely White shorthairs were bred and shown by Lady Glubb, whose husband, Sir John, was Glubb Pasha of the Arabian affairs of the 1939 war.

There is a tradition (mentioned, incidentally, in the Gordon Stables book) that white cats were favoured by millers, since they did not show against the flour bags. This pre-supposes that they could deceive the rats and mice who were the miller's enemies by merging with their background; it suggests a picture of the rodents, unable to see their predators, and apparently not noticing scent or sound of them either, falling easy victims to the miller's policing white cats!

Blacks

Standards for colour in Black shorthairs are:
Governing Council:
Colour: Jet black to roots, no rusty tinge. No white hairs anywhere.
Eyes: Deep copper or orange with no trace of green.
   Rusty tinge permissible in kittens.
Nose leather: Black.
Pads: Brown or black.
Withhold certificates: Incorrect eye-colour. Green rims.

The Cat Fanciers' Association:
Colour: Dense coal black sound from roots to tip of fur. Free from
   any tinge of rust on tips or smoke undercoat.
Nose leather: Black.
Paw pads: Black or brown.
Eye colour: Brilliant gold.

The American Cat Association:
Black: Rich, lustrous black, sound to skin.
Eyes: Copper. Deeper shades preferred. Full 10 points deducted
   for green eyes. Undesirable: white hairs, rusty belly or rusty
   ruff. Smokey ruff or undercoat. *White spots disqualify.*

Two difficulties arise in the breeding of the exhibition 'Blackies':

there is apt to be discoloration of the coat, and the eye-colour may be incorrect. Breeders have the difficulty of waiting for their kittens' eyes to change, and this can take a fair time and requires patience. The kittens at birth have, it is said, 'blue eyes'; this, however, is not the clear sky-blue of, for example, the Siamese eyes, but a very dark blue. It occurs, now and then in human infants; someone will say of a brown-eyed child 'He was born with blue eyes'. What is meant is an appearance of 'navy blue' in a dark eye which, in a human baby, soon changes to brown or hazel. In kittens, the blue does not long remain, but the colour stays indeterminate sometimes for weeks. Breeders of Burmese find that the kittens' eyes are likely to be a bad colour: the lovely yellow of the eyes of an adult Burmese of quality will not yet have appeared in a young kitten. Similarly, the eyes of a domestic shorthair kitten may appear 'muddy' and it can be a long time before the breeder of a little family of Black kittens can be certain that the eyes are truly orange or copper, and have no green at all in them.

The matter of coat-colour is as important: the operative clause in the standard of points is 'rusty coat permissible in kittens'—for the kittens with the rusty coats are likely to become the adults with the best jet black pelage. 'Rusty' is the right word for the colour concerned: it in no way resembles the red of a Self-Red or Red Tabby; it is, as it is said to be, a rusty tinge at the proximal part of the hairs of a Black kitten, and it will fade with the passage of time, and leave a coat that is jet-black and more sound in colour than is, very often, found in the cats who had, as kittens, no rust in their coats.

White in the coats of show Black cats is a serious matter. The British Governing Council standard states unequivocally 'No white hairs permissible'; the American Cat Association states 'Undesirable: white hairs' and adds '*White spots disqualify*'. This last is undoubtedly an echo of the tendency for 'common-or-garden' cats, the 'moggies' of long ago, to be either Tabbies or Black-and-White cats.

Standards in the USA insist upon one more aspect of coat-colour in Black shorthairs. CFA directs 'Free from... smoke undercoat.' And ACA, under its undesirable characters, lists 'Smokey ruff or undercoat'.

The 'ruff' is of course the 'frill' of the exhibition longhair, but the smokey undercoat may occur in a shorthair, and it is important to appreciate the difference between a Black Smoke (Chapter 4) and a Black cat whose show potential is spoilt by an undercoat of down hairs that have developed a greyish tinge. It is not, fortunately, a very common fault; and there is no more handsome shorthair than the champion Black whose fur is jet-black to the roots, and whose round, big, copper eyes regard the world like twin Hunters' Moons.

4

Standards and Varieties: III

Smokes

The Smoke cats are best described in the words of their standards, and in their particular case it has to be remembered that the first exhibition Smokes were longhairs. The Governing Council standard for the shorthair Smokes runs:

Colour: Black or blue. Undercoat pale silver.

Eyes: Yellow or orange.

Nose leather and pads: Blue or black to correspond with coat colour. (Kittens should not be penalised for ghost markings.)

Faults: White guard hairs. Over-long coat.

Withhold certificates: Incorrect eye-colour. Tabby markings. Over-long coat.

To evoke a mental picture of the beginnings of this variety, it is worthwhile to give the British (Governing Council) standard for colour and coat in the longhair Smoke:

A Smoke is a cat of contrasts, the undercolour being as ash-white as possible, with the tips shading to black, the dark points being most defined on the back, head and feet, and the light points on frill, flanks and ear tufts.

Colour—body: Black shading to silver on the sides and flanks. Mask and feet: black with no markings. Frill and ear tufts: silver. Undercolour as nearly white as possible.

Coat: Silky texture, long and dense, extra long frill.

Eyes: Orange or copper in colour, large and round in shape, pleasing expression.

The above is also the standard for Blue Smokes except that where the word 'black' occurs, 'blue' should be substituted.

This standard gives a very good description of a most spectacular cat. The length and quality of the fur and the unusual colour distribution combine to produce one of the most striking coat patterns. The shorthair Smoke, without the advantage of the longhair's flowing coat, is less arresting in appearance; but he is a very pretty, unusual cat and, whereas his British standard is brief, in the USA the Cat Fanciers' Association standard, under its list of 'American shorthair colours', gives this variety a more detailed description:

Black Smoke: White undercoat, deeply tipped with black. Cat in repose appears black. In motion the white undercoat is clearly apparent. Points and mask black with narrow band of white at base of hairs next to skin which may be seen only when the fur is parted. Light silver frill and ear tufts.

Nose leather: Black.

Paw pads: Black.

Eye colour: Brilliant gold.

The CFA standard for the Blue Smoke is of course identical with that for Black Smoke, with the substitution of 'blue' for 'black'.

The American Cat Association gives its shorthair colours as 'Colour shall be as described in Persian colour standards.' For the smoke longhair, the ACA colour description reads:

Black Smoke: The Smoke cat shall have a black top coat shading to grey on stomach, with a pure white undercoat. Mask and feet black but with white undercoat. Frill and ear tufts pale silver. Eyes: copper. Undesirable: white spots or hairs, or black locket, grey topcoat or dingy undercoat, marked shading or bars. *No Tabby markings allowed.*

Blue Smoke: Substitute blue for black in the above description. Frill and ear tufts are white.

The ACA standard makes a distinction between the Blacks and the Blues, ascribing silvering to the former, and white to the latter. This undercoat, however, is probably due to the gene for silvering. ACA also gives firm emphasis to the undesirability of Tabby markings. It should be noted that the word 'frill', so apt a description for the splendid ruff of the exhibition longhair, is not really appropriate to the shorthair, but is used in some of the standards with reference to the fur of the neck; the meaning is clear, although the shorthair Smoke does not possess the frill which is the 'colerette' of the European longhair. In fact, this is one 'silvered' exhibition cat not ancestrally connected with Silver Tabby: informed opinion is that the Smokes were originally bred from Blacks, Blues and Whites. 'The Smoke... is thought to have originated by the mixed breeding of Blacks, Whites and Blues'.[1] Silver Tabby is never used in breeding Smokes—obviously it would bring in the undesired markings. In the USA, Red Smokes, known as Cameo Smokes, are recognised.

Smokes are rare, but they are still to be seen, and breeders say that successful litters can be expected if a Black stud is used; it is of course possible to mate Smoke to Smoke, but too many such matings will result in loss of type.[2]

The Smoke factor may become evident in unexpected places: it appears in Cornish Rex; sometimes a Rex cat will have underfur of the ash-white colour proper to a Smoke; I have myself a young Cornish Rex given to me by Mrs Hetty Hamilton, a Blue kitten of show quality. He was about two years old when I saw that the fur behind his ears looked silver. He is, in fact, a Blue Smoke, with down fur and the proximal ends of the hairs ash-white: similar coats have been seen in the show pen. The cats concerned are not shorthair Smokes within the definition of the standard: my young neuter is of show quality as a Cornish Rex—but not by any means as a Smoke! He has an ash-white undercoat, but it cannot be described as 'tipped with blue', nor has he a 'light silver frill and ear tufts'. In fact, such Rex cats are not Smokes at all within the meaning of CFA's excellent standard—nor, indeed, of any show standard.

Yet their ash-white underfur is produced by the factor responsible for exhibition Smoke cats. It is a factor not always welcomed by breeders. There have been complaints that Red and Cream longhairs showed white in the undercoat and this, of course, is not desirable in show cats. It does not, however, necessarily have any connection with the 'ash' undercoat produced by the silver factor. It does not do to forget that man never achieves anything in the cats that nature unaided could not have produced. He breeds, by careful selection, a Smoke cat exemplifying the standard which he has drawn up, but the gene which governs the Smoke character may affect feline coats without our intervention. It is the silver gene that is the operative factor and its action is interesting. 'Keeler and Cobb have shown that the gene producing "silver" or "smoke" in cats is an allele of the same gene which produces the Siamese coat pattern.... The effect of silver is variable, and may produce hairs of several sorts: (1) all white, (2) all black (in dark silvers or smokes), (3) black hairs with white tips, (4) hairs with white and grey or black bands, and (5) white hairs with black tips'.[3] So that what the Cat Fancy has done is simply to select the effects that pleased it best, so producing the Smoke cat of exhibition quality.

Bi-colours

The Bi-colour is another cat of unusual beauty; with big patches of colour and white, he presents a striking appearance. These cats have been bred, of course, from the 'moggies' of years gone by. There have always been cats of no pedigree who were Tabby-and-White, Red-and-White, Blue-and-White and, in particular, Black-and-White; there were always plenty of Black-and-White and also, as an exhibitor recently remarked, of White-and-Blacks, that is, with White predominating. Colour standards for exhibition Bi-colour shorthairs are given as follows by the Governing Council:

Colour: Any accepted colour and white. The patches of colour to be clear and evenly distributed. Not more than two-thirds of the cat's coat to be coloured and not more than one half white. Face to be patched with colour. White blaze desirable. Symmetry in design is desirable.

Eyes: Brilliant copper or orange.

Faults: Brindling or tabby markings.

Withhold certificates: White patching on solid colours. Incorrect eye colour. Green rims.

Bi-colours are not listed in the standards-of-points for the Cat Fanciers' Association nor the American Cat Association, but the Cat Fanciers' Federation and the Crown Cat Fanciers' Federation give a description under *Parti-colour:* Parti-colours are cats combining any of the colours listed and white with no more than two-thirds of the cat to be any one colour.

Tortoiseshell-and-White cats are sometimes spoken of as Bi-colours, though they are in fact of three or four colours: as the British standard has it: 'Black, cream and red on white, equally balanced. Colours to be brilliant. The tri-colour patchings should cover the top of the head, ears and cheeks, back, tail and part of the flanks. Patches to be clear and defined. White blaze desirable. Eyes should be copper or orange. Nose leather and pads as for Tortoiseshell.

Faults: Tabby markings. Brindling. Colour unbroken on paws.Unequal balance of colour. White must never predominate; the reverse is preferable.

Withhold certificates: Incorrect eye-colour. White predominating. Green rims.

In the USA these cats are called Calicos, and CFA, under American Shorthair Colours, gives *Calico*: White with unbrindled patches of Black and Red. White predominant on underparts. *Eye colour:* Brilliant gold.

The American Cat Association has: *Tortoiseshell-and-White:* same as for Tortoiseshell, except legs, throat, belly and nose should be white.

The Tortie-and-Whites are extraordinarily lovely in Britain, where a breeder of distinction, Miss Woodifield, has devoted herself with great success to the task of bringing them to perfection.

The Blue-Creams whose coat-colour is the dilution of the Black-Red of the Tortoiseshells have the corresponding 'Blue-Cream-and-White' standard. When nature takes a hand, such cats can be beautiful: I have seen two Blue-Cream-and-White kittens in the country not far from Oxford who would, with their clearly-defined patches of colour on white, have been a credit even to such a breeder as Miss Woodifield.

Cream occurs in the Black-and-Red Tortoiseshells and Tortoiseshell-and-Whites: the patches of red and its dilute as well as black, on white, make the beautiful four-coloured coats of these cats.

Manx

Manx have covered themselves with glory as show cats: at the Governing Council's Supreme Show in 1979, the Supreme Best Adult was Grand Champion Tatleberry Long John, bred by Mrs Hellman and a son of Grand Champion Tatleberry Tashmetum. I had the pleasure of awarding Tash's second Grand Challenge certificate in 1975, and certainly he and his descendants are most beautiful creatures, conforming splendidly to the standards.

In the 1960s, there was in Britain a Manx called Empress, owned by Mrs Earnshaw, a cat of very high quality. At the Ulster Cat Club's Show in Belfast in 1978, Best-in-Show by common consent of all the judges present was another Tatleberry Manx, registered as Dirty Digby; the name did not seem appropriate, for he was beautifully groomed and in grand condition! In the USA, also, Manx have been very successful show cats: the *Cat Fanciers' Association Year Book* for 1978 lists in its regional awards a Bi-colour male Manx, Oniga Lemminkeine, as fourth best in the top ten for Gulf Shore: while the pictures of the Grand Champions for that year include Wyola Joel of Hyacinth and Miskini's Casper. There is also in the Year Book an advertisement for Tynwald Manx with a picture of a Brown Tabby Manx who—although it is not right to judge cats from pictures—looks extremely lovely.

The Committee of the Short Haired Cat Society has agreed a new provisional Standard of Points for Manx, and this has not yet (September 1980) been submitted to the Governing Council. The principal change asked for is for *Body:* Solid, compact, with good breadth of chest and short back ending on a definite round rump, the rump to be higher than the shoulder. Flanks of great depth. At present the Council asks for:

Scale of points

Taillessness	25
Coat texture	15
Head and ears	15
Body and shape	25
Eyes	5
Shortness of back	10
Condition	5
Total	100

Head: As near to British as possible. Fairly round and large with prominent cheeks. Appearance, rather jowled. Nose longish without a definite nose break but with no appearance of 'snipeyness'.

Ears: Wide at base, tapering slightly to a point. Taller than standard British and set more on top of head.

Eyes: Large and round. Colour corresponding preferably to British standard colours.

Body: Solid, compact, cannot be too short and ending on a definite round rump. Back legs higher than front, making an incline from back to front. Flanks of great depth.

Legs: Of good substance with front legs short and well set apart to show good depth of chest. Back legs longer with a heavy muscular thigh.

Coat: Short, good texture. Double coated showing a well padded quality arising from the longer outer coat and the thicker undercoat. Coat colour and markings only taken into account when other points are equal.

Tail: Absolute taillessness is essential in a show specimen and there should be a decided hollow at the end of the backbone where, ordinarily, the tail would begin.

Faults: A rise of bone at the end of the spine. A non-visible joint or cartilage.

Withhold certificates: Definite visible tail joint. Incorrect number of toes.

The Cat Fanciers' Association:

Manx point score

Head and ears	10
Eyes	5
Body	25
Depth of flank	5
Taillessness	10
Shortness of back	5
Legs and feet	15
Coat	15
Condition	5
Colour and markings	5
	100

Head: Fairly round with prominent cheeks and jowly appearance. Medium in length without a definite nose break.

Muzzle: Tapering, but not to a sharp point.

Ears: Rather wide at base, tapering slightly to a point and longer than those of the American shorthair, but in proportion to the head.

Eyes: Large, round and full. Points to be divided equally between size and colour.

Body: Solid, compact and well balanced, with the back showing a definite incline from the shoulders to the haunches. Small or medium in size. 'Bunny-like' in appearance.

Flank: Of great depth, adding to the cobbiness and balance.

Taillessness: Absolute in a perfect specimen. A decided hollow at the end of the backbone where, in the ordinary cat, a tail would begin.

Back: Sturdy and short, to conform with the actual size of the well-balanced cat.

Legs: Of good substance, with front legs short and well set apart to show good depth of chest. Back legs much longer with a heavy, muscular thigh tapering to a substantial lower leg that often has the hair worn off due to the fact that the Manx rests on this part as often as on the paws.

Paws: Small, neat and well rounded with five toes in front and four toes behind.

Coat: Short, of good texture, with a well padded quality arising from the longer outer coat and the thicker undercoat, known as a 'double coat'.

Condition: Good physical condition. Muscular, good flesh but not fat.

Penalise: A rise of the bone at the end of the spine. A non-visible joint or cartilage.

Withhold winners: Definite visible tail joint. Incorrect number of toes.

CFA gives a list of Manx colours; these include the accepted shorthair colours—White, Black, Blue, Red and Cream, with descriptions as under the CFA standards for domestic shorthairs; and also chinchilla, shaded Silver, Black Smoke and Blue Smoke, with descriptions as under CFA Persian standards for colour.

The American Cat Association:

Scale of points

Ears	10
Eyes	5
Body	25
Taillessness	40
Coat	10
Colour and markings	5
Condition	5
	100

Only cats scoring 85 or more points are eligible for winners.

Head and ears: The head should be fairly round with prominent cheeks, especially in the males. The nose should be slightly longer than the domestic shorthair, with no suggestion of snipishness, and straight when viewed from the side. There should be a whisker break and prominent muzzle. The ears are medium in size, rather wide at the base and taper gradually to a rounded tip. They are rather widely spaced and set slightly outward.

Eyes: 5 points

Large, round and full. Colour of secondary importance

Body: 25 points

Cobby, with a short back with rump high and well rounded. Flanks elongated. Neck short and thick.

Taillessness: 40 points

The Manx cat must be free from *any trace* of tail. There is a dimple where the coccyx ordinarily starts.

Coat: 10 points

Open or 'double' coat with woolly texture. Short thick undercoat with slightly longer outer coat.

Colour and markings: 5 points

All colours, including parti-colour, eligible for winners.

Condition: 5 points

Good physical condition. Muscular but not fat.

Several points arise from these standards; they are pretty well in agreement; and they all ask for a short back. The British Standard states that the back 'cannot be too short'—but not all breeders will be quite happy with this. 'I do not think the very extreme rumpy i.e. with *very* short back, is the ideal proposition for breeding'.[4] This well-known and highly-successful breeder goes on to say that her preference is for 'a sturdy, well-balanced cat' for breeding, and this reflects the simple common sense that is the basis of all healthy breeding, and which requires, among other reasonable pre-requisites, that the female pelvis shall be of a size to accommodate comfortably her young *in utero* (Chapter 5). Writing in *The Manx Cat*, in Manhattan, Mrs Marion Hall wants Manx to be 'medium in size, not too large or too small,' and another writer, Mrs Mary Stewart, agrees with her. It has been said that loss of fur on hind legs is 'due to the fact that the Manx rests on this part as often as on the paws'; I have not seen this manifestation nor, indeed, seen any cat resting on a *leg*; all cats, including Manx, walk upon their 'tippity-toes', and when they sit down, the whole hind foot, from toe to heel, rests upon the ground, as do the ischial tuberosities; it may be that Manx cats place the whole foot, from toe to heel, on the ground more often than do other felines.

Manx cats have been talked of as unusual and discussed with interest for a very long time. They are spoken of by fanciers as rumpies, i.e. the cats with complete taillessness asked for in the standards; and as 'stumpies'—those with a tiny stump of a tail, unacceptable as contenders for championship honours; there are also indigenous to The Isle of Man tailed British shorthairs. Informed opinion has it that the tailless condition originated as a mutation in the domestic shorthair.

Mrs Hellman tells us in a valuable paper that research into the history of these cats was meticulously carried out by the late Dr Kerruish. He it was who established the cattery on the Isle of Man, much visited by interested tourists, though its cats are not always such beautiful examples of the variety as are seen in the show-pen. The Canadian Manx and Cymric Society magazine has a comment by Blair Wright, who visited Man, that the cattery is lovely, but the inmates poor. The Hellman paper tells us that there have been stories of tailless cats in the Crimea. But Dr Kerruish believed that the mutation in the domestic shorthair that produced the tailless cat occurred in the early eighteenth century, *circa* 1730; he bases this belief on the facts that it was at this period that the Manx language fell into disuse, and that there is no Manx word for the tailless cats: plainly, if the tailless cats had been present in the Island while its native tongue was used, the Manx language would have included a word for them.

The Governing Council in Britain has recently (1968) dropped mention of the 'hoppity gait' once thought proper to Manx from its standard; it has been found that this 'bunny-like' manifestation is caused by a defect that makes it difficult for the cat to move its hind legs independently. It has for long been considered that the tailless condition in this cat is a deformity, and connected with various defects; the Hellman paper makes clear that if only perfectly sound individuals be used for breeding, then these cats will be as healthy as any other variety—and as strong, in fact, as the domestic shorthairs in whom the mutation for taillessness occurred (Chapter 5).

It may perhaps be noted that these cats breed successfully in free populations in farmland and countryside; in Australia, indeed, a wandering Siamese stud and a Manx female have been responsible for the arrival of a 'Si-Manx'. This, of course, is not a particularly desirable occurrence in the matter of 'breeding to the standard', but it suggests good health, and it is certainly true that there are cats with perfect health who measure up well to their standards. It is said that in the USA longhair Manx have been bred by fanciers; Mrs Batten points out the curious fact that such a cross has never been reported as occurring in nature.

Tipped cats

The Tipped cats recently making their debut at shows are the shorthair version of the Chinchillas. They have been bred from a Chinchilla and Silver Tabby cross (Chapter 5) and have for some little time been shown in Britain in assessment classes: that is, in classes for new breeds not yet with a breed number of their own, so that senior judges may assess them according to their provisional standard, a copy of which is attached to the exhibit's show cage. Judges are asked to answer 'yes' or 'no' to the question 'Merit Awarded?'. In Britain, the Tipped cats, recognised by the Governing Council, have achieved (1980) their championship status.

It may be thought that no shorthair could ever attain the spectacular beauty of the Chinchilla; but the Tipped cats at their best, silvered and sparkling, are exquisitely pretty. The Governing Council Standard of points for British Tipped cats reads:

Scale of points	
Head	20
Eyes	10
Body	20
Legs	10
Tail and paws	10
Coat and condition	30
	100

The general conformation to adhere strictly to that laid down for the established British shorthair breeds.

Colours: Tipping to be of any colour accepted in the recognised British breeds, with the addition of brown, chocolate and lilac.

Coat: The undercoat to be as white as possible. Coat on the back, flanks, head, ears and tail tipped with colour. This tipping should be evenly distributed to give a sparkling effect, and it is the even distribution of the tipping rather than the degree of tipping which is of paramount importance. Heavily tipped cats must not be penalised so long as they are free of markings, in fact they are preferable to the cats which carry so little tipping that they appear almost white. The legs may be very slightly shaded with tipping but the chin, stomach, chest and undertail to be as white as possible.

Nose leather and pads: In all colours, nose leather and pads pink or corresponding to colour of tipping as near as possible.

Eyes: Cats with black tipping should have green eye colour, otherwise eye colour to be orange to copper.

Faults: Any tendency towards foreign type to be considered a very serious fault. An orange rim in a green-eyed cat, or a green rim in the eye of an orange eyed cat. Tabby markings or spots in the coat colouring with the exception of vestigial tail rings, which should not penalise an otherwise good exhibit.

In the USA these cats have long been established. The Cat Fanciers' Association standard for their colour is precisely the same as this Association's colour standard for Chinchilla, and both the longhairs and the shorthairs have the same name—Chinchilla. Their standard reads:

Colour: Undercoat pure white. Coat on back, flanks, head and tail sufficiently tipped with black to give the characteristic sparkling silver appearance. Legs may be slightly shaded with tipping. Chin and ear tufts, stomach and chest, pure white. Rims of eyes, lips and nose outlined with black.

Nose leather: Brick red.

Paw pads: Black.

Eye colour: Green or blue-green.

The Crown Cat Fanciers' Federation gives, under 'Description of Colours' for domestic shorthairs, Manx, Longhairs and Rex:

Chinchilla Silver: Undercoat, pale silver white, coat on the back, flanks, head and tail sufficiently tipped with jet black to give the characteristic sparkling silver appearance (of an overall pearl coloured cat). Legs and face may be very slightly shaded with tipping, but the chin, ear tufts, stomach and chest should be silvery white without tipping. Rims of eyes, lips and nose to be outlined in black.

Eyes: Blue-green.

Nose leather: Brick red.

Paw pads: Dark charcoal or black.

Objections: Any barring on face, legs, body and tail; cream or brown tinge in coat, yellow or hazel eyes.

Faults: Blue tipping is a severe fault.

This Federation includes also, under longhair and shorthair colours, the Shell Cameo, which is the Red-tipped counterpart of Chinchilla, and directs:

Shell Cameo: Ground colour, frill, ear tufts of ivory white, shaded with red tipping on head, legs, back and tail so as to give a sparkling peach ice cream colour to the overall cat.

Objections: Tabby markings; pale or lemon eye colour.

It was predictable that red should be introduced by experimental breeders to produce a red-tipped coat and in this they have conspicuously succeeded. Though the Red-tipped cats are not at present (1980) recognised by the Governing Council of the Cat Fancy, there is a proposed standard of points for them as longhairs, and its direction for colour, which presumably would apply to shorthairs, reads:

Shell Cameo: Characteristic sparkling silver appearance lightly dusted with rose-pink. Nose leather and pads pink.

It had also been foreseeable that shorthair breeders would make use of the gene for silver to obtain a counterpart to the Chinchilla; and although the 'Chin' has a coat that seems like moonlit mists, unsurpassed for beauty in any breed, yet the best of the Tipped cats have in their pelage the brilliant sparkle which silvering brings.

Scottish Folds

There are other varieties of British shorthairs; not everyone will have made acquaintance with Scottish Folds, those tough little Highlanders with ears folded over like the flaps of 'pochette' handbags. Yet there are pictures of them in the *Cat Fanciers' Association 1978 Year Book*; and I saw some, including a fine litter of three-month-olds, in Australia in 1977. It has been thought that the folded ears must impair the cats' hearing, and thus be a defect. However, it has to be taken into account that these cats have without trouble maintained themselves in the wild; this they could not have done if they had been unable to hear the approach of predators; and indeed, although mine is only a layman's opinion, it did not appear, in appraising these cats, that the folded pinna occluded the passage to the inner ear. It has been said that the Folds can, if the spirit moves them, raise their folded ears to stand upright. No official standards of points are (1980) available for the Scottish Folds, who only appear at shows as being of interest; but it is probable that they may in the course of time be accepted, since the minutes of an executive meeting of the Cat Fanciers' Association, given in their *1978 Year Book*, includes: 'Scottish Fold. The following standard is presented for your consideration: "The Scottish Fold cat occurred in a spontaneous mutation in farm cats in Scotland. The breed has been established by crosses to British shorthair and domestic cats in Scotland and England. In America the outcross is the American and British shorthair. All *bona fide* Scottish Fold cats trace their pedigree to Suzie, the first fold-ear cat discovered by the founders of the breed, William and Mary Ross.

Head: Well rounded with a firm chin and jaw. Nose to be short with a gentle curve. Muzzle to have well-rounded whisker-pads. Head should blend into a short neck. Prominent cheeks with a jowly appearance in males.

Eyes: Wide open with a sweet expression. Large, well rounded and separated by a broad nose. Eye colour to correspond with coat colour.

Ears: Fold forward and downward. Small, the smaller, tightly folded ear preferred over a loose fold and larger ear. The ears should be set in a caplike fashion to expose a rounded cranium. Eartips to be rounded. No matter how dramatically folded the ear, if the whole cat presents an overall appearance contrary to the standard for the whole cat, type must prevail.

Body: Short, rounded and even from shoulder to pelvic girdle. The cat should stand firm on a well padded body. Legs medium in length and in proportion to the body. There must be no hint of thickness or lack of mobility in the cat due to short coarse legs. Toes to be neat and well rounded with five in front and four behind. Overall appearance is that of a well rounded cat with medium bone. Females may be slightly smaller.

Tail: Tail should be medium to long but in proportion to the body. Tail should be flexible and tapering.

Coat: Short, dense and resilient.

Disqualify: Kinked, broad, thick or foreshortened tail."'

When acceptance of this standard was moved, it was carried, and this, at an executive meeting of an important governing body, augurs well for these healthy, attractive cats.

Rex

Rex cats are also domestic shorthairs, and for them there is championship status. They were not 'discovered' by the cat fancy until the 1950s, when Cornish Rex, fostered by Mrs Ennismore on farmland, were brought by Dr A. G. Searle and Mr Jude to the attention of the late B. A. Stirling-Webb. Their waved fur is due to a mutation occurring in the domestic shorthair, and standards have been drawn up for them as follows by the Governing Council:

Cornish Rex
Scale of points

Coat	35
Whiskers and eyebrows	5
Head shape	15
Eyes	10
Ears	10
Body and legs	20
Tail	5
	100

Coat: Short and plushy, without guard hairs, and should curl, wave or ripple particularly on back and tail. Whiskers and eyebrows crinkled and of good length. All coat colours acceptable, but any white markings must be symmetrical except in Tortoiseshell-and-White.

Head: Medium wedge. Head length about one-third greater than the maximum width, narrowing to a strong chin. The skull to be flat. In profile a straight line to be seen from the centre of forehead to end of nose.

Eyes: Oval shaped, medium in size, colour in keeping with coat colour.

Ears: Large, set rather high on head, wide at base, tapering to rounded tips and well covered with fine fur.

Body and legs: Body hard and muscular, slender and of medium length. Legs long and straight, giving an overall appearance of being high on the legs. Paws small and oval.

Tail: Long, fine and tapering, well covered with curly fur.

Devon Rex
Scale of points

Coat	40
Head	15
Eyes	5
Ears	10
Body, legs and back	25
Tail	5
	100

Coat: Very short and fine, wavy and soft, without guard hairs. Whiskers and eyebrows crinkled, rather coarse and of medium length. All coat colours, except Bi-colours, acceptable. Any white markings other than in Tortoiseshell-and-White will be considered a fault.

Head: Wedge-shaped with face full cheeked. Short muzzle with strong chin and whisker break. Nose with a strongly marked stop. Forehead curving back to a flat skull.

Eyes: Wide-set, large, oval shaped and sloping towards outer edges of ears. Colour in keeping with coat colour or, except in Si-Rex, chartreuse, green or yellow.

Ears: Large, set rather low, very wide at base, tapering to rounded tops and well covered with fine fur. With or without ear muffs.

Body, legs and neck: Body hard and muscular, slender and of medium length, broad in chest, carried high on long slim legs, with length of hind legs emphasised. Paws small and oval. Neck slender.

Tail: Long, fine and tapering, well covered with short fur.

The deeply-waved coat of a Rex of high quality is the singular and very beautiful distinguishing character of this breed, and it will be noted that very high marks are allotted for coat, as being the most important feature of these cats. The late B. A. Stirling-Webb who, with some of his American friends, established these cats, believed that there would eventually be only one standard for them and, in fact, most USA governing bodies give only one.

It is sometimes thought that Cornish Rex cats are foreign, but this is because it was decided by the committee that drew up their first standard that they should have a medium wedge head and long, slender legs. The cats have of course been bred to this standard, although it should be noted that their heads are of only *medium* length, and they have not lost all the sturdiness of their British shorthair ancestors; they were found in England, in Germany and in Oregon: and their beautiful coats are due to a mutation which occurred in domestic shorthairs in the USA, in England and in Europe: this is made abundantly clear in the preamble to the Cat Fanciers' Association's Rex standard, which states that the Rex cat is a spontaneous mutation of the domestic cat, and gives the standard as follows:

Head: Comparatively small and narrow; length about one-third greater than the width. A definite whisker break.

Chin: Strong, well developed.

Cheeks: Lean and muscular.

Muzzle: Narrowing slightly to a rounded end.

Nose: Roman. Length is one-third length of head. In profile a straight line from end of nose to chin with considerable depth and squarish effect.

Eyes: Medium to large in size, oval in shape and slanting slightly upward. A full eye's width apart. Colour should be clear, intense and appropriate to coat colour.

Ears: Large, wide at base and come to a modified point at the top. Placed high on the head and erect.

Body: Small to medium, males proportionally (sic) larger. Torso long and slender. Back is arched with lower line of the body following the upward curve.

Shoulders: Well knit.

Rump: Rounded, well muscled.

Legs: Very long and slender. Hips well muscled, somewhat heavy in proportion to the rest of the body. The Rex stands high on its legs.

Paws: Dainty, slightly oval. Toes, five in front and four behind.

Tail: Long and slender, tapering towards the end and extremely flexible.

Neck: Long and slender.

Bone: Fine and delicate.

Coat: Short, extremely soft, silky and completely free of guard hairs. Relatively dense. A tight, uniform marcel wave, lying close to the body and extending from the top of the head across the back, sides and hips continuing to the tip of the tail. The fur on the underside of the chin, and on chest and abdomen is short and noticeably wavy.

Condition: Firm and muscular.

The Cat Fanciers' Association adds to this highly-detailed standard a list of Rex colours, described as for North American Shorthairs; they are White, Black, Blue, Red, Cream, Chinchilla, Shaded Silver, Black Smoke, Blue Smoke, Cream Tabby, Tortoiseshell, Calico, Blue Cream, Parti-Colour, all varieties of Tabby and ORC (other Rex colours). Calicos are Tortoiseshell-and-White cats, and the Smokes are a manifestation of the gene for Silver, with the hairs as described in the CFA standard, so deeply tipped that the cat in repose appears black or blue, whereas in movement the ash-white undercoat is clearly apparent.

For the important coat, 40 points are allotted both by CFA and by the American Cat Association, whose Rex standard reads:

Head: 10 points

Should be longer than it is wide with a break at the muzzle when viewed from the front. A straight line should be from the top of the nose to the chin.

Neck: 5 points

Neck should be medium long and slender.

Ears: 5 points

Ears shall be large, set high on head, taller than they are wide with a modified point at the top.

Eyes: 5 points

Eyes shall be medium size, oval in shape, a colour in keeping with the coat colour is desirable, but secondary to the overall appearance of the eyes.

Tail: 10 points

Tail shall be long and slender, tapering slightly from the body to the end.

Body: 10 points

Tuck-up: Body shall be long, slender, with 'tuck-up' behind the ribs and hips somewhat heavy in proportion to the rest of the body. Body must be hard and muscular, medium to small in size, with fine bones.

Legs: 5 points

Legs are long and slender in keeping with the type of body and tail. A Rex cat is high on the legs with feet that are dainty.

Coat: 10 points

Coat should be short and dense.

Waviness: 10 points

A coat with deep even waves is desirable, especially on the back and tail. Coat on head and tail shall be texture of velvet pile.

Colour and markings: 10 points

Colour and markings are as for the Manx cat.

Condition: 5 points

Firm and very muscular.

Balance: 5 points

Viewed as a whole, the cat shall be well knit, smooth and each part in good proportion.

    This detailed description describes well the little Rex, who is one of the more recent arrivals on the 'show' scene; the Cornish Rex is strong and healthy, and worthy to take his place where he belongs: among the foursquare, natural British, American and European shorthairs.

5

Genotypes

In considering the evolution of *Felis domesticus* and the mutations which have brought about changes in him, it is important to remember that man has never altered, and never could have altered, the genic material already present.

Sir Julian Huxley states that evolution proceeds by small, discontinuous variations; and sometimes in an organism, a gene mutation will take place—a genotypic change which will alter the phenotype: a clear example is the recently discovered change to wavy hair found in the Rex cat. Such changes, however, can only occur naturally. The French philosopher Lamarck believed that circumstances in the life of an individual could alter the constitution of the progeny, but this is not the case: if a man's foot is cut off, he will still pass on to his children the gene for bi-pedality.

However, man's comparatively recent interest in cats has brought rapid change in their phenotype: an experimental breeder works with the material already present—the factors in the cat's gene-complex. He never achieves anything that nature unaided could not have brought about; but when he takes a hand, he becomes a selective agent for the breed concerned. He discovers what factors are present, and makes use of them, by controlled matings, to accentuate whatever characters are of interest to him. He can never alter the genic material, but he greatly hastens the process of change. This is less evident in the domestic shorthair than it is in some other breeds.

The type of the Siamese cat has greatly—and quickly—altered as a result of man's intervention, and so has the head of the Persian, and the length of his coat. The domestic shorthair, however, has not very much changed; it is true that the household cat of the early 1900s had sometimes a slightly pointed face, whereas the show shorthair of the mid-century has a round face; indeed, it has recently been suggested that breeders of shorthairs were tending to select for a facial conformation reminiscent of the somewhat exaggerated, even peke-faced type of the show longhair. However, the shorthair champions of today have usually the round head and strong jaw and chin which their standard demands, and in fact, the type admired by breeders is the deep-chested, cobby, firm conformation that is natural to these cats, and makes of them a very healthy breed. (Chapter 6).

Man's prerogative of choice is well-exemplified by the fairly recently approved Rex cat; an *ad hoc* committee, convened to frame a standard to be put before the Governing Council, was asked to consider whether Cornish Rex should be bred with heads of round, British type, or with heads of 'foreign' conformation. Two members of the committee, one an Australian lady, would have preferred British type; they were outvoted but, fortunately, *modified* foreign type was decided upon, and the standard asks for a *medium* wedge head. The requirements of the Fancy were achieved by breeders in the usual manner: the age-old time-honoured method of breeding like-to-like; individuals with tall legs and medium length of head were mated together, and the kittens best conforming to the man-made standard were kept to be bred from, and exhibited, and given awards by judges, so that the Cornish Rex of today have kept their beautiful coats and do not have round heads. The manner of their very recent breeding is a good illustration of the speed with which man, as a selective agent, can influence the course of evolution. A little more support for the two people who favoured British type at an afternoon's committee meeting, and the Cornish Rex of today might all have round faces.

Such committee decisions can have a world-wide effect, for throughout the twentieth century Australia and New Zealand have tended to agree with and to use British standards. The United States and Britain have worked together since the days of Lady Marcus Beresford and Mrs Clinton-Locke of Chicago and, later, Mrs Virginia Cobb; and the standards of points of the two countries, though not precisely similarly worded, tend to have the same meaning, and the same desiderata for exhibition cats.

Coat colour and pattern

From time to time surveys have been carried out to discover the incidence of coat-colour and pattern in the domestic cat: Dr Searle inaugurated one such in London some years ago, and in Australia in the 1960s, Mrs Mary Batten assisted Professor Bruce Moffat in such a survey; and it was found that Black-and-White predominated. Indeed, the shorthair Black-and-White Bi-colour has always been very much to the fore in free cat populations, and among household pets. Yet it is the Tabby who has the original, wild-type coat-pattern. Khunying Abhibal Rajamaitri, the Thai lady who is a well-known cat-fancier, writes that 'The common-or-garden cat in Bangkok is the Tabby'; and the patterning of stripes, spots or blotches is almost impossible to eradicate from the feline coats. A black pelage seen in brilliant sunlight will sometimes show the ancient pattern, like a shadow or a piece of shot-silk, so that the eye seems to see two depths of blackness.

The persistence of tabby in the cat has never been overcome; in non-Tabby pedigree cats, fanciers have wished to eliminate it, and have drawn up standards accordingly, demanding for this or that breed that there shall be 'no stripes' or 'no shadow markings'; the usual show routine has been followed: if a shadow pattern shows in one of two exhibits otherwise of equal merit, then the judge will place his rival above him; and so breeders will select for mating cats that have no tabby. Yet that faint shadow pattern will show, perhaps on the flanks, appearing now and then even in the pale coats of Siamese.

It is not easy to get rid of ancestral characters that have been of use in the wild; and the colouring and patterning of the Brown Tabby cat has always had strong survival value: it has given him protection against his predators by enabling him to merge with his surroundings in bush and forest; and it has also had threat value against his enemies by helping to make him, as his hairs rose in fear or fury, a terrifying sight.

Tabby and agouti are not the same thing; they are independent, and are seen in the Tabby cat as a grey-brown ground of banded hairs (agouti hairs) 'on which may be superimposed a pattern of spots, stripes or blotches.'[1] The word 'agouti' is taken from the name of a South American rodent whose coat is made up of banded hairs. In the melanocyte (pigment cell), which secretes the pigment granules, a change occurs from eumelanin to phaeomelanin, showing in agouti hairs as black and yellow. The same melanocyte may be able to secrete one or the other granule, and the change may be due to a switch mechanism; melanocytes of every agouti genotype can produce both eumelanin and phaeomelanin. The independence of tabby and agouti is exemplified by the fact that although the O (yellow) of the Fancy's red coat-colour is epistatic over agouti, yet the pattern of tabby superimposed upon the agouti ground of hairs banded in black and yellow occurs in Red cats as well as in Blacks. The significance of this is that if yellow and agouti were alleles of the same gene, the dominant yellow would, in the Reds, prevent the agouti from appearing in the phenotype. The independence of the two genes allows both to show, producing the beautiful patterning that we see.

The Red Tabby has the yellow of the agouti banded hairs as background and, superimposed upon it, the deep, rich red pattern governed by O. It has to be remembered that red in the cat has the peculiarity of being sex-linked. The gene for red is carried on the X chromosome, and not on the Y, and in addition, it is dominant in the male kittens and partly dominant in the female kittens.

Genes exist in pairs and are carried on the chromosomes, of which the X and the Y are the sex-determining chromosomes: every female carries XX and every male XY; these sex chromosomes are present in the gametes—the ova and the spermatozoa; so that each ovum carries X and each sperm either X or Y. At fertilisation the pairs of chromosomes are restored, the new zygote—in this case the kitten—receiving an X from the dam, and from the sire either X or Y. If the kitten is XX it will be female, if XY, a male.

The genes, carried in a definite linear order on the chromosomes, are responsible for all the characters in an organism and, in *Felis domesticus,* the gene for red coat-colour is sex-linked: that is, it is carried on the X chromosome and not on the Y, besides being dominant in the male kittens and partly dominant in the female kittens.

Thus a mating between a Red male and a Black female will produce no Red males, since the kittens will receive Y, not carrying O, from their sire, and X from their non-yellow dam. Whereas to the fancier a 'ginger cat' is a red, he is yellow to the geneticist; however, the symbol O (orange) was decided upon by a nomenclature committee for the factor concerned because Y for yellow would cause confusion with the Y chromosome.

The female kittens from the Red male-Black female cross will all be Tortoiseshells, since they will receive X, carrying red (partly dominant in the female kittens) from their sire, so:

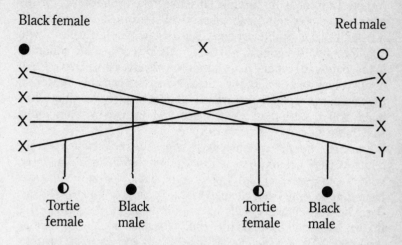

Black female

Red male

Tortie female | Black male | Tortie female | Black male

In the case of a mating between a Black male and Red female, the sons, receiving X with dominant red from their dam, will all be red, and the daughters, since in them red is only partly dominant, will once more be Tortoiseshell:

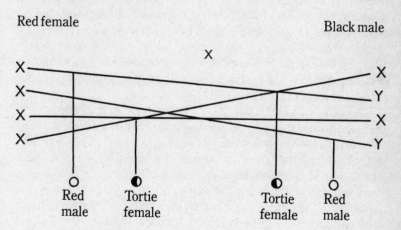

Red female

Black male

Red male | Tortie female | Tortie female | Red male

If, however, one of the Tortoiseshell kittens be mated to a Red male, Red females may result, as well as Red males, since they will receive O from both parents. This sex-linked inheritance of the gene for red accounts for the absence of 'Tortoiseshell Tom' which puzzled Gordon Stables at early shows: the gene for yellow, with only incomplete dominance in the female kittens, is fully dominant in the males, so that any male kitten who receives it will have a coat of full colour and be a Red; whereas his sisters can only be Reds if they receive O from both parents. Thus it is likely that more Red males will be born than Red females, and this is why it is so often said that 'a ginger cat is always a Tom'.

Cream in the cat's coat behaves as does the red of which it is the dilute. A Blue-Cream is, genetically, a Tortoiseshell in dilute form, with cream carried on the X chromosome and not on the Y. It has from time to time been claimed that a Tortiseshell male has been born; but these have usually been infertile; it has been suggested that such a kitten could be the result of a genic imbalance, making the kitten XXY, but in general, male kittens acclaimed as Tortoise-shells turn out to have coats of vari-coloured Tabby. It is in any case probable that a kitten born with a genic abnormality would be infertile. There is in fact one authentic recorded instance of a fertile male Tortoiseshell: this was a Rex cat named Poldhu born in 1955, bred by Mrs Ennismore, who registered him with the Governing Council, and owned by Mr Stirling-Webb. This cat was said by some people to be 'some sort of Tabby', but he was seen by Dr Searle, who said that he was a dilute Tortoiseshell (Blue-Cream), and pointed out that he sired red and cream female kittens to four different queens, a thing that could only happen if he carried O, for which the X chromosome would be the vehicle.

The beautiful Tortoiseshells, extensively bred and especially in England where they are fostered by a breeder of distinction, Miss Woodifield, are lovely in the Bi-colour form, Tortie-and-White; and a Tortoiseshell may have in her coat the three colours, red, black and cream, in clearly-defined patches; this gives red and its dilute, both present in the same cat's coat, a phenotype not found, for instance, in the case of black and its blue dilution. Sir Arthur Keith tells us that 'every gene is affected by the action of every other gene', and modifying factors may always be present.

Where red or cream coats are concerned, those most admired at shows are the very pale cream and the deepest red: obviously,

between the palest cream and the darkest red, there is a very wide
range of shades.

Manx cats

A cat whose genetic background has been extensively discussed is
the Manx. Mrs Jane Hellman, who is our best authority on these
cats, and who has described them in a valuable paper (Chapter 4),
tells us that the mutation became evident about 250 years ago on
the Isle of Man, and that litters will consist of kittens with tails—
often very long tails—with stumpy tails of varying lengths, and
with no tails at all, known as 'rumpies'; these last, of course, are the
ones eligible for show. The expected ratio of tailed kittens to Manx
from a Manx × Manx mating is 1:2, and the fully-tailed kittens do
not carry the gene for Manx. This mutation occurred in British
shorthairs and although tailless cats have now and then been
spoken of in Europe, it is clear that the best place for the
establishment of any form of speciation is always an island, a closed
enclave for breeding.

It has often been supposed that the tailless condition of these cats
is a defect; and indeed, FIFE (Federation Internationale Feline
d'Europe) has, in Sweden, banned Manx, and has said it is wrong to
keep the breed going: 'the taillessness being a distressing
congenital defect bred purely for showing which means misery and
death for many of the cats'.[2] It has been thought that to cross rumpy
with rumpy for more than one generation will result in disaster, in
the form of infertility, 'fading' kittens and the like; Mrs Hellman has
not found this to be the case and she points out that, as in any breed,
healthy, normal parents will have healthy descendants. She states
that she herself breeds from healthy stock, with width of body, and
that her queens kitten easily, and rear healthy kittens. It is probable
that many judges would bear her out, for plenty of healthy Manx
cats, many of them of her breeding, have appeared at shows. She
makes the point that any kitten not perfectly healthy should be
neutered as a pet and this is true of all animals—no sub-standard
individual should be bred from.

It ought to be remembered that nothing can be better than a small
in-breeding community *provided the original genes are healthy* (Sir
Arthur Keith). The Hellman paper stresses the absurdity of
supposing, as some have done, that one gene can be responsible for

lack of tail, shortness of back, length of hind legs and softness of the double coat in Manx cats. This of course cannot be seriously entertained. Pairs of genes govern all the characters in an organism, and every gene is affected by the action of every other gene; characters may be modified by such action, but it can never be maintained that the same allelomorph is responsible for—as an example—length of hind legs and softness of coat.

Breeding is always a matter of common sense; for show, shortness of back is considered proper to these cats, but, quite simply, a female with *too* short a back may well not have enough space for a growing litter. Exaggeration is always to be avoided. Incidentally, Mrs Hellman tells us that the 'hoppity', rabbit-like gait looked for in Manx, and which has now been removed from the Governing Council standard, is in fact due to a defect, and should not be present; Manx cats, however, because of their long hind legs, can run like hares (Chapter 4).

There appears to be no good reason why lack of a tail should in itself be thought to constitute a defect. Man has no tail, although his ancestors of millennia ago probably had. It should be noted that the gene responsible for taillessness in Manx has no connection with that concerned with kinks in the tails of Siamese.

Man's desire for experiment has produced longhair Manx, and nature, aided by a Siamese 'escapologist' and his immediate descendants in Australia, has achieved a Si-Manx. It appears more than likely that there is no lethality in these cats, and it must be frustrating for their breeders that 'To investigate the mechanics of Manx inheritance the scientists have...generally used abnormal cats in their experiments. Through this they produced more deformed cats'.[3] Common sense suggests that this is like arranging a marriage between two deaf-mutes and then claiming that mankind suffers from a congenital defect.

Tipped cats

The Tipped cats, recently making their appearance in Britain and the USA, are the shorthair version of the Chinchillas, and have been bred from a Chinchilla-Silver Tabby cross. The silver factor, in the Chinchillas and longhair Silver Tabbies and in the Smokes, both long and short haired, comes originally from the shorthair Silver Tabby, and its expression in the Chinchilla is extremely beautiful; the flowing white hairs, tipped with black, give the effect of silver gauze. It was predictable that fanciers would produce a shorthair with like expression of the silver gene — the Tipped cat.

Intermediates

Cats with long fur have for a very long time been present in the West; among the non-pedigree population, there have been individuals whose fur was longer than that of the usual 'moggie' shorthairs, though their coats had not the tremendous length of the carefully bred pedigree cats, who were, at the beginning of the present century, imported from Persia and from Turkey. In an article in the Colourpoint, Rex-coated and AOV Club's Journal, Robin Sims makes the point that whereas the terms 'Persian' and 'Angora' are often used interchangeably, the cats concerned are not the same: the flowing coats of the cats brought to Europe from Iran are not governed by the same gene as that concerned with the cats imported from Ankara. This writer makes it clear that the present-day Turkish Van cats are Angoras, and holds the opinion that it was unfortunate that in the early 1900s the Angoras were used to improve the coats of the Persians. It must certainly be accepted that an Angora, originally a white longhair brought from Turkey, is not the same variety of cat as the Persian.

The prized 'fluffy cat' appearing in the native populations was referred to by fanciers as an 'intermediate'; it is the considered opinion of breeders that the show longhairs of today are descended from such 'intermediates' with, most probably, some crossing with the Persians and Angoras imported from Iran and Turkey; and Mary Batten holds the view that it is an open question whether the fluffy cat-on-the-sidewalk got his pretty coat from the indigenous Scottish wildcat, or maybe from cats brought from the middle East by the Romans. 'Almost certainly the factor which has produced the 'fluffy' coat is common to both sources'.[4] These cats have been present in the west for much too long to owe their provenance to recent imports; and the patterning of their coats has always had its counterpart among the shorthairs; it is certainly not surprising that fanciers have wished to breed a shorthair version of that extremely lovely manifestation of the gene for silver, the Chinchilla. The 'Chins' are immensely popular on both sides of the Atlantic: Lady Haden-Guest speaks of seven or eight recent imports into Britain from the USA. And there is probably a brilliant future for the Tipped cats who have in 1980 achieved championship status in Britain (Chapter 4).

Mrs Batten relates that in 1967 a Tabby-point male bred by her was mated to a Chinchilla, and produced kittens whose fur was of intermediate length, and 'tipped'; a second family could, of course, have been all shorthairs. And, given the agouti factor (Chinchilla) which is dominant, the tipped effect can be produced in a coat of any colour—as red. Such cats are designated 'Cameos'; they are of course shorthair Chinchillas with the factor for red.

The varieties newly recognised as show cats by governing bodies are often spoken of as man-made, and this is a misnomer, since man can achieve nothing in the cats that nature unaided could not have produced. However, what man can do is to select this or that feature as desirable and, by careful breeding programmes, encourage the appearance and continuance of the character of his choice. 'We speed up evolution.... It isn't that man creates, but just that he operates with the variations that occur' (the late A. C. Jude). This places a heavy responsibility on man, for it sometimes gives rise to an exaggeration not conducive to health. An example is the narrowing of the face in Siamese: because the suggestion of length in the heads of these cats was pleasing to the people who fostered them, the standard drawn up for them asked for a long head; and this feature has, by selective breeding, been so much exaggerated that some of the cats have narrow, snipey faces, with very small lower jaws; it is even said that some breeders in the USA have had teeth extracted from Siamese cats in order to make their heads appear narrower. The longhair too, with his width of head and tiny nose, has often occluded nasal ducts and an overshot jaw. Thus man, exaggerating natural features, sometimes fails to put good health first.

The British, North American and European shorthairs have been fortunate: the people who have bred the domestic shorthair for show have admired in him the very characters which are natural and strong: the round head, the sturdy body and limbs. Of all exhibition cats the domestic shorthair is, with the possible exception of Burmese, the one who has best kept his natural conformation.

6

Care and Health

Health is more important than anything else and domestic animals are, in this century of rapidly-advancing knowledge, reaping the benefit of their attachment to man. Many of the most valuable advances which modern science has made concern medicine and hygiene. Medical research has been carried out for most species and vaccines have been produced to protect the cat from such feline ailments as the distempers once grouped together as 'cat flu' or 'feline infectious enteritis'.

Immunisation

Owners of cats and kittens owe it to them to see that they are immunised against the ills that threaten them. It is true that the cost of vaccination is high: but the protection which it gives is of enormous value, and a great deal of work, equipment, and expenditure has gone into the production of vaccines. In addition, no one who cannot afford the time or the money to care properly for a cat ought to own one; to look after a cat properly should include giving him the benefit of all the protection that is available.

It is best to let the vet.-surgeon decide at what age a kitten should be vaccinated; products vary, so that sometimes one 'jab' is enough, and sometimes a 'booster' is necessary. Furthermore, medical research is not static, and with constant new knowledge, procedure alters as the years go by. Veterinary surgeons are always apprised of new discoveries; a vet.-surgeon may be attached to a hospital or to a research station, and in any case he will have read the latest journals concerned with his profession, and will have discussed new discoveries with colleagues; and his opinion will be worth having.

Veterinary care

In this connection, it is well to realise that the opinion of a layman has never the same value as that of a qualified person. Where the matter of nursing a sick animal is concerned, a fellow animal lover's advice may be very helpful: he may have found a way of administering medicine to a recalcitrant pet that is worth a try by someone else caring for a sick cat, or he may have discovered some soothing way of grooming staring fur; an ailing cat will often purr with gratitude if someone gently cleans and tidies his coat. However, in diagnosing or treating a condition, what a kind neighbour thinks, or can tell about 'exactly the same illness' in his or her own cat, is not really valuable; the best advice that can be given is: if your cat is out-of-sorts and remains so for more than a day, get veterinary help. Of course, the agitated owner who rings up a busy vet.-surgeon because little pusskins has refused one meal probably has only nuisance value! The cat may simply have eaten a vole and not be hungry! Cats seldom, in fact, eat the small rodents or—alas—birds which they kill; but it can happen, and it can make the cat refuse a regular meal though he is perfectly well. Any change in the usual behaviour-pattern may, however, spell trouble; it is best to watch for a few hours and, if there is still something wrong, to seek qualified advice. If there is, after all, nothing much the matter, no harm will have been done; but if there is trouble, it will be an advantage for it to be dealt with early.

There must, perhaps, be some element of risk in taking a cat to a surgery waiting-room, for this is a place where sick animals have a right to be, and many disease germs are air-borne; but it can often be arranged with the receptionist that the cat may wait in the car, in his own hamper, until his turn comes, and be taken straight into the consulting-room. To ask the vet.-surgeon to visit the patient at home is expensive, for veterinary costs have risen as have all others in the worldwide monetary recession of the late twentieth century. It is by no means always necessary to ask for a visit; but sometimes it may be essential as when, for instance, a queen has trouble kittening; and whatever is advisable for the cats, we ought to give them, for they have thrown in their lot with us, and we have accepted them; so that it is our duty to provide for them all the benefits that our knowledge has gained.

Where health is in question, the domestic shorthair has a very good start. In an article in *Purr,* the official publication of the Feline

Association of South Australia, of November 1977, I wrote that the British shorthair is 'a strong, sturdy creature, deep-chested and powerful....These are very healthy felines, for they are as nature intended them to be, and have not had their appearance organised out of recognition by controlled breeding'. And indeed, these cats have not had their lower jaws weakened as has happened in Siamese, sometimes bred for extreme length of head so that they are, as described in France, 'Surtypés'. Nor have they occluded sinuses as have some longhairs, bred for shortness of nose and breadth of face. 'Their whole conformation makes for health and strength. The females, with cobby bodies, are fit to carry healthy litters, as the strong males are to sire them'.[1] There seems no reason to change this opinion.

It is true that in his breeding experiments the fancier has, in the domestic shorthairs, chosen for breeding the cats with the most roundness of head; the slight pointedness of the face in the earlier shorthairs has thus given way to the full cheeks and rounded contours of the present-day show cats; longhair breeders of distinction will say that they can detect in the Chinchillas and other Persians who carry the silver gene a slightly pointed facial contour, not like the extreme breadth of face of some longhairs, and inherited from their Silver Tabby ancestry. Many shorthair Silver Tabbies are, however, appearing at shows with the admired round heads; but no one, mercifully, wishes to alter the strong body with its depth of chest and its thick legs. The British/North American shorthair thus remains a very healthy breed.

Fanciers tend to discuss feline illnesses and these are sometimes said to affect particular breeds; it is interesting that the many conditions talked of are rarely said to affect these shorthairs.

The drawings in the Gordon Stables book of last century show the slightly pointed faces present in the cats of the time, both long and short haired. There are in this book many passages which read absurdly in the light of later knowledge, yet the author gives a good deal of sound advice; he advocates making grass available for the cats—something not always understood by town-dwellers to be desirable. And he knows that 'cats nearly always prefer water to milk when they are really thirsty.' This last is, indeed, something not realised by every cat owner: there are still many people given to saying 'Milk is there natural food'. This is only true in the sense that all the mammalia start their lives with their dams' milk; how would a cat in the wild obtain cow's milk? This author, himself a vet.-surgeon, appreciated the importance to health of good, natural conformation: in this connection, he writes of the Brown Tabbies as 'True English cats'.

Rabies

Nowadays, reputable breeders will not send their kittens to new homes until they have been vaccinated. Besides the F.I.E vaccine, there is available immunisation for cats against rabies, that dreaded condition so dangerous to man and beast. In the matter of this scourge, anyone taking or sending a cat to another country should find out about the current situation. In the USA there are no quarantine laws; in Europe there are very strict laws. As recently as 1979, a lady wishing to take a kitten from Britain to France was told that if the kitten arrived at a French port without a certificate of vaccination against rabies, the Douane would have him destroyed. I was asked to enquire into this, and found that it was by no means true: a cat or kitten taken to France from England was required to have the normal veterinary certificate of health needed for any country, and issued shortly before export, and, in this case, made out in both languages; and either a certificate of vaccination against rabies, or a letter of clearance from the Ministry of Agriculture and Fisheries. If the kitten arrived in France without the latter, he would be required to be inoculated before he could be cleared by the Douane; but he would certainly not be destroyed. In view of possible alterations and very strict laws, the proper procedure for anyone exporting a cat or kitten is to get in touch with the Ministry of Agriculture and Fisheries, whose headquarters (1980) is at Surbiton, Surrey, telephone: 01-337 6611. Ask to be put through to the department dealing with the export of cats, and give the name of the receiving country and any other information asked for. The Ministry will send all appropriate instructions and forms, and their requirements are very easily carried out. But it must be remembered that conditions—and therefore rules—can change. For one thing, the length of the quarantine period varies according to the incidence of rabies: in Britain, if the country has been rabies-free for a long time, the quarantine period will be comparatively short; but if there should be a case of rabies reported, the cats will have to be kept longer in quarantine; further, rules and regulations may be changed in any country at any time. Therefore, when either importing or exporting a cat, it is always wise to get in touch with the Ministry so as to obtain the very latest information.

Rabies is so serious that rules have to be stringent: it can kill off a herd of deer, can—as hydrophobia—affect man, and is rightly dreaded throughout the world. Britain, with strict measures and with the advantage of being an island, has succeeded well in keeping herself rabies-free. The disease is dreaded in Europe, and France, whose researches and vaccines have been of enormous help, is rightly also very strict. It is not surprising that French quarantine regulations should be severe, for France, through her great scientist Louis Pasteur, handled superbly the terrible problem of rabies; until comparatively recently, a man bitten by a rabid dog had to go to Paris for treatment at the Pasteur Institute. In Australia, the greatest care is taken, and cats are more readily accepted from Britain than from central Europe.

A cat in quarantine is not necessarily unhappy. At Shurlock Row Quarantine Cattery near Henley, I have seen the little prisoners looking very plump and prosperous, with everything provided for them, including grass growing in large boxes of earth. And the huge, wonderfully-equipped quarantine station at Perth in Western Australia is beyond praise: its kitchens alone are worth a visit and beautifully organised. Obviously, any animal would prefer freedom to restraint, but no animal could be unhappy in the conditions at this recently-founded and perfectly-run station: the cats and dogs sojourning there are in splendid condition, and no loving owner need have any anxieties.

De-clawing

In any fancy, there is bound to be controversy, and recent points of disagreement include the question of de-clawing (onyxectomy). In any difference of opinion there will be two views; in the matter of removing a cat's claws, the argument in favour is that the claws catch and pull and tear the threads in valuable furnishings. The argument against de-clawing is that it is mutilation which leaves the cat unable to defend himself against attack, or to escape danger by climbing a tree. In fact, no one who has seen the horrified dismay of a maimed cat who jumps up, maybe onto a chair-back, and falls for lack of the means to hold on, could possibly be complacent about this horrible mutilation. Admittedly, a cat—naturally given to stropping his claws—has no place in a room where there is furniture of great value. But those whose living-rooms contain such furnishings ought not to keep a cat at all. Some people possess lovely antique furniture which they keep in the 'state apartment' from which their cats are excluded; anyone who wants to live with valuable tapestry cannot reasonably live with cats as well; for to de-claw them is to mutilate them. No cat who has been de-clawed may be entered in a show run under Governing Council rules, nor under the rules of the CFA and other American governing bodies.

De-vocalisation

It is also possible, for people who do not like the sound of a cat's voice, to have him 'de-vocalised'. It is to be presumed that owners of Siamese are those who approve this operation, for the longhairs and domestic shorthairs have tiny voices which probably could not be an annoyance to anyone. Mrs Glenda Hubbard of the Oxford Cat Club tells a charming story of her unregistered Black-and-White cat, who goes for walks with his owners, conversing softly as he walks along. Many years ago, I had a Brown Tabby who came walking with my children and me, but he did not speak to us; however, I know that Mrs Hubbard likes to hear Poco's soft voice. It is of course true that the Siamese voice is very loud indeed. A calling Siamese queen literally roars—and incessantly. Her shouts can be a great annoyance to breeders and to their neighbours. Even the ordinary, brief remarks of a Siamese are uttered loudly; and the breeds ancestrally connected with the Siamese have voices louder than the little 'mew' of a British or North American cat; a Burmese, for example, though not producing anything comparable with the Siamese roar, has a deeper voice than the western cats.

Those who really love cats will consider that it is disgraceful to operate upon a cat's vocal chords for the convenience of his owners since, except for reasons of health, interference with nature is never good, and those who do not like loud voices in cats would do better not to own Siamese. So far as the British shorthairs are concerned, their very soft voices are probably not at risk.

8 Cream kittens owned by Mrs Brown. (Photo: Anne Cumbers)

9 Blue Cream owned by Mrs Brown. (Photo: Anne Cumbers)

10 *Top* Champion Brynbuboo Betsy Gay, bred by P. Absalom,
owned by P. Stephens. (Photo: P. Stephens)

11 *Above* Grand Champion Brynbuboo Ben Buckley, bred by P. Absalom,
owned by J.N. Stephens. (Photo: P. Stephens)

12 *Left* Champion Brynbuboo Betsy Gay. (Photo: P. Stephens)

13 *Left, below* Woad Caractacus. Blue owned by Mrs Lynn Murphy. (Photo: P. Stephens)

14 *Below* Panda's Blue Flower. Blue owned and bred by Mrs Elmers. (Photo: Hetty van Winsen)

15 *Below* Black cat bred and owned by Mrs Irwin. (Photo: David Irwin)
16 *Right* Smoke kitten owned by Mrs Memezes. (Photo: Anne Cumbers)

17 *Top* Pathfinders Meg. Tortoiseshell-and-White bred and owned by Miss Woodifield. (Photo: Anne Cumbers)

18 *Above* Pathfinders Mavis. Tortoiseshell-and-White bred and owned by Miss Woodifield. (Photo: Anne Cumbers)

Monorchidism

Trevor Turner, M.R.C.V.S., was a member of the panel at the Teach-in held by the Russian Blue Cat Society in the Spring of 1980 in London, and although the little 'Russkis' who are, incidentally, beginning to regain their characteristic fur and the depth of green in their eyes, are foreign shorthairs and were, of course, the main subject for discussion, Mr Turner told the audience several things of general interest. It is always good to have a vet.-surgeon on such a panel; for judges present can most usefully discuss and assess the show points of the cats, but questions concerning health are nearly always asked from the body of the hall, and a judge, unless he has veterinary qualifications, cannot authoritatively answer them.

In Auckland, during 1977, at a seminar, I was billed as the principal speaker, and I was happy to talk about the show qualities of the cats, and about their breeding and their heredity; but there was present a vet.-surgeon, Mr Lifton, who answered the many questions which concerned feline health, and he seemed to me to be of major importance, for to cat lovers, the well-being of their animals matters enormously, and what a vet.-surgeon has to say is always of interest to them. Mr Turner, whose work is at the Mandeville Veterinary Hospital, at Northolt, told the Russian Blue Teach-in something not always properly understood; under Governing Council rules, and also under CFF rules and others in the USA, a cat who is a monorchid may not be shown. People are inclined to think of a monorchid as a cat or kitten in whom only one testis has descended into the scrotum, and to suppose that the other 'may come down later'. However, in fact a monorchid is a cat in whom only one testis is present—the second is missing. A cat or kitten in whom both are present but only one is in its correct place would be a crypt-orchid.

Showing kittens

Another point of controversy recently discussed is the question of the age at which a kitten may be shown. Governing bodies throughout the world have a rule that a kitten may not be entered at a show until he is four months old. The relevant Governing Council show rule is 'The minimum age for kittens...is four months', and it is almost identically worded with that of the Cat Fanciers' Federation: 'Any...kitten not less than four months old....'

Requests have been made recently that the rule should be altered to allow the kittens to be exhibited at three months; but it is not likely that there will be any change, for there are good reasons for this rule. Kittens will continue to take milk from their dam until they are three months old, and often a little longer, continuing even when they are eating solid food, provided supplies are plentiful; and the more milk is taken, the more there will be. Thus, given a strong queen and a litter of hearty 'good-do-ers', they will attach themselves to her furry waistcoat 'just for a snack', until they are quite big. Under the rules of the various governing bodies, a lactating queen may not be shown so that, in order to exhibit a three-months kitten, it is necessary to separate him from his dam and, if she still has milk, those who advocate showing at three months, may be heard to say 'I shall wean him'.

Unless the queen is out of condition, it is not right for the breeder to decide when a kitten shall be weaned. Solid food can usefully be offered to a litter at a very early age: it is a good idea to offer it (perhaps tiny scraps of raw beef) as early as four or five weeks, protecting it from the queen, who will certainly eat it up if she gets a chance! The kittens will not at first accept it; and their dam can be allowed to have it; but sooner or later, one of the kits will pick up a bit and find it good, and very soon they will be crowding round the dish, stamping on each others' faces to get the most. Their acceptance will depend upon the amount and quality of the maternal supplies, but as they grow, the kittens will need more and more to supplement her milk, and so by three months, nature will be starting to wean them.

So long, however, as the queen has milk for her kittens and they are taking it, and however much else they may be having in the way of extra supplies, it is a mistake to separate them: for they get from her not only an extra feed, but an immunity from various conditions which may beset a cat. To take them arbitrarily from her is to deprive them of this protection. It is never wise to run counter to nature. The best way is to provide plenty of good food for both the queen and her kittens, and to let her feed them just as long as she has good milk for them. Of course it can happen, even in a strong breed, that a queen's supplies may run out early; it is important for the breeder to watch the kittens and see that they are getting milk, and are growing; if there should be trouble, it will be necessary to hand-feed the kittens or to find a foster-mother, preferably with veterinary advice. But given a healthy queen with a healthy litter, it is best to let nature take care of the final weaning—by four months, it will be accomplished.

Thus there is very good reason for the decision not to show a kitten under four months old; and unfortunately for those who want this rule changed, there can only be one reason for showing a kitten at three months, and that a desire to sell the kitten. There are, alas, some who grudge the money and time spent in feeding and caring for kittens, and think of breeding only as a money-making exercise.

In fact, breeding, properly carried out, has never been cheap, and is less so in times of monetary inflation; food, upkeep of housing and appurtenances, veterinary bills, are all a consideration. Of course, prices of pedigree kittens have also risen. But breeding pet animals is not a commercial proposition, and for those who love them, it is a labour of love.

Hand rearing

To rear a litter whose dam has come to grief is not an impossible task. A mixture made up of one teaspoon cow's milk to two teaspoons water with a little sugar added, warmed and administered with a dropper every two hours will simulate the natural maternal milk, and the kittens will take it easily. As they grow, the feeds can be strengthened with yolk of egg, and the kittens will soon discover the dish that holds the food, and start lapping for themselves. At first, of course, they must be fed through the night, but the hours between meals can gradually be lengthened. They will cling to the person feeding them, and there is a drawback to be faced when they discover the dish and start lapping: for them, the natural manner in which to take the maternal milk would have been to lie face down against their dam's furry waistcoat; and when they start to feed for themselves, their instinct is to lie down in the dish, so that, as the late B. A. Stirling-Webb said, 'You spend your time washing the kittens'. But they soon learn.

Kittening

It is important to see that a queen has plenty of good food while she is carrying her kittens, and also while she is nursing them. As a rule, cats will kitten without difficulty, purring the while; and a well-built, well-fed British shorthair is likely to produce her family without trouble; but since it is possible for things to go wrong, it is best to keep an eye on any queen when she goes into labour; leave her in her box, her basket, or wherever she or her owner has decided she shall kitten, but look in on her from time to time. If contractions continue for a long time without result—that is the danger signal, and qualified help should be sought. Difficulties are the exception rather than the rule: it is good to have the vet.-surgeon's telephone number handy just in case; but usually, a healthy shorthair will very soon be joyfully purring over a family of strong little good-do-ers.

Parasites

There are sundry items in caring for cats, whether as pets or for breeding, which can be attended to without recourse to professional advice. Intestinal parasites are easily tackled in most cases; roundworm (ascaris) must be dealt with if they are present: most breeders will give tablets to all their cats every three months whether any signs of worms have been seen or not. Roundworm will not do serious harm to an adult cat, but if neglected they can kill a kitten. Very often, they are brought up from the stomach, or they may be observed in the 'scratch-trays'. Anyone who keeps many cats will be well advised to consult his vet.-surgeon as to what vermicide—or vermifuge—to use, and then to keep his cattery clear of these disagreeable parasites by administering regular doses at stated intervals. *Coopane* can successfully be used; it may be given to a queen in kitten, and it can be powdered into the cat's food: it will not be noticed, since its only taste is a faint saltiness. A tablet given to each adult, and a quarter-tablet to each kitten will be effective; and a second dose given eight to ten days after will clear away any eggs that may have been left behind. It is, however, important to have a word with the cats' own 'doctor', for if he has their health in his care, then his instructions should always be carried out, both as to what preparation to use, and as to intervals between doses. There is also a possibility of tapeworm; these may be observed as small white segments in the excreta. They are not regarded as dangerous to the cat, but they must be got rid of in the interests of hygiene. Here again, a vet.-surgeon will advise as to the best remedy to be used.

There are, of course, many conditions that can affect the cat: skin troubles alone are numerous, and any sign of a little 'crusty' patch needs professional opinion, for the layman will not know which of many conditions is present; and there are some, as ringworm, that can affect man. However, such afflictions are rare, and not difficult to treat when they do occur.

Care of the ears and eyes

There are small routine aids to well-being that can be dealt with at home without running to the surgery; ear-mites are common as a cat becomes old, and 'ear-drops' can be provided through the vet.-surgeon, most conveniently put up in small 'squeezy' bottles, so that they can be pressed straight into the ear. These mites can lead to intense irritation, head-shaking, and violent scratching; they are, however, first evident as an ear that looks dirty, with dark, sticky little patches inside the pinna; so that a careful owner who inspects his cats as he grooms them will observe them as a 'dirty ear' long before the scratching stage is reached, and will be able to use the drops as provided by his professional adviser.

Eyes require great care: if they should become 'sticky', it is perfectly possible that the matter can be dealt with by using a small tube of *Golden Ointment*, or of whatever preparation the vet.-surgeon has recommended: if the infection be mild, or is simply due to age, it will not be necessary for the vet.-surgeon to see the cat every time his eye is a bit sticky in the corner; but if the situation worsens, or the preparation used is not effective, then there is need for advice.

Cat fleas

Another pest to be guarded against is the cat-flea. These infest the coats, particularly of young kittens in warm weather, but to an extent of all cats if the matter is not attended to. However well-scrubbed a cat-house may be, these little fleas establish themselves, often in the cracks between floor-boards, to infest the coats of cats and kittens. The reputable firms market good powders to deal with the situation, and here again it is easy to organise matters so that a cattery is kept clear of fleas. Rub a very little powder lightly into the coats of kittens and their dam, just once a day, from their birth, particularly where the tail joins the back, and there will never be any fleas.

It is worth knowing that neither worms nor fleas are of the same kind in cats and in man; they are not interchangeable, and the parasites that thrive in the cat will not establish themselves in his owner.

Geriatrics

It is sad that the lives of our cats are comparatively short. Sixteen years is a good age for a cat, although many are reported as living longer. For a cat who has lived a healthy life and whose race is run, the end may come suddenly, within a few weeks, with inability to jump up onto a lap or a chair, maybe with failing sight, so that he has to grope for his food. It is possible to ask the vet.-surgeon to come and give him a little prick, maybe as he lies on his owner's lap. He will not know. We, who have loved him, owe it to him to 'talk him down' cheerfully, in the voice he knows, so that he is never unhappy. In a cat who lives his full span, very often, as he becomes really old, the kidneys will be affected; he will drink a great deal of water, and be always hungry, yet nourishment will not reach the tissues, so that he will be very thin. If he is in no pain, his vet.-surgeon may decide to treat him, and such treatment can be successful, but only to a limited extent. The cat may enjoy his existence, eat very well, go out into the sunshine and lie dozing under a hedge. But once he can no longer be happy, when there is nothing more for him, then it may be best to make sure that he does not suffer on his way to the happy hunting grounds.

7

Pets and Neuters

It is as pets that cats have their greatest charm. They have been treasured by many people who never heard of the Cat Fancy, and who never connected their loved malkins with money. It is, however, fair to say that many breeders keep their queens and their studs and care for their kittens for love of the cats rather than for profit: stud-owners of note have said 'I love my boys', and fanciers whose circumstances forced them to cease breeding have exclaimed sadly 'I do miss the kittens.'

It is an unfortunate fact that there are people who breed kittens for the hope of monetary gain, or for personal advancement as judge of this or that breed, or as chairman of some committee. But for the most part, the people who foster pedigree cats do so for love of felines, and there is no reason why a breeding queen should not be her owner's pet companion as well as a good mother. Very big prices are asked and paid for show quality kittens; this has to be so, for everything connected with breeding has become more costly, as is the case with most activities. Stud fees, veterinary accounts, food, repairs to housing, accessories—everything the cats need has become more expensive and a breeder cannot afford to sell his kittens cheaply. Still, it is very often the case that his brood queen is also his loved pet, and that he feels real pleasure when his famous stud, arrived at the end of his career, can be neutered and come indoors where as one owner said 'He is so *happy!*'

The matter of neutering pet cats is important. It is not possible to keep an entire male as a pet; to try to do so is to court disaster. A whole male, charming though he was as a kitten, cannot be a suitable inmate for his owner's home. He will spray walls and furnishings, leaving a most undesirable scent, and this is his nature—something for which it would be quite useless to scold him. He will go out at night and will fight with other tom-cats: while he is young he will win his battles, but as he grows older, younger cats will be the victors, and he will become a battered, scarred, wretched-looking creature.

Buying cats and kittens

When it comes to buying a cat or kitten as a pet, many people want their new friend to be a good-looker; most breeders can sell a kitten who fails in some show quality less expensively than his better-looking sib—usually with the proviso that he shall be neutered. Neutering is, however, in any case desirable for a pet. The RSPCA and the Cats' Protection League (Chapter 9) are both institutions that may with advantage be contacted by someone seeking a pet cat. The CPL, for instance, cares for cats and kittens who have been lost or even abandoned, until homes can be found for them. There are unfortunately many instances of pedigree cats turned out when people who had paid a high price for a fashionable animal grow tired of them. Siamese and Persians and beautiful British shorthairs are often to be found at the homes of officers of the CPL, being cared for until they can be well placed. The League will give such a cat to a suitable owner 'free for nothing', but will ask the new owner if he can afford a subscription. Obviously the rescued cats cannot be taken good care of without expenditure, and it is hoped that those accepting the cats will make a contribution according to their means. Of course, such a pet will not have a known pedigree; unsuccessful efforts will have been made to find his previous owners, but nothing will have been found out. Still he may be just what is wanted: a lady once asked me if I could find her a ginger cat; I rang the nearest CPL representative and— it seems incredible!—there was available a beautiful, young Red male. This lady gave a good subscription and everybody was happy, including the cat, who had the curious distinction of being a British shorthair with a permanently bushed-out tail!

Whether a pet cat or kitten is obtained from a breeder or from a charitable institution, the important thing is to make very sure of his health and, if his antecendants are unknown, to consult a vet.-surgeon about the matter of inoculation; it is important for kittens to have their 'shot' and, if there is a possibility that this may already have been attended to, then it is best to have professional advice: the vet.-surgeon will know when an inoculation—which may be a second one—can be given.

Neuters

The only way to keep a stud is to provide him with a house and garden of his own, where he may receive visiting queens, and play host to his own queens, and be well fed, and kept from living 'rough'. A queen, when she is not nursing her kittens, can be the charming house-pet she has always been, but if a male is to be a pet cat, he must be neutered. This operation is slight, in no way tiresome, all over in a few minutes, and the cat, taken indoors to be petted and loved, will be the happier for it.

Not that a cat kept for stud is unhappy; he will get plenty of visitors, plenty of good food, and excellent premises. Years ago, a stud-owner used to give her boy a raw egg, which he loved, every time he mated a queen; he very soon understood the routine, and when he was entertaining a visiting queen, he could be heard shouting 'Where's my egg?' or sounds to that effect. It is not really necessary for a stud to be lonely; often two may live together; it seems improbable that two entire males can share the same premises, but many have done so, particularly cats who were father and son.

To spay a female is a bigger operation than to neuter a male, but it is easily and successfully carried out by reputable vet.-surgeons, and a spayed queen is a delightful companion for someone who loves cats but is not able to undertake the work of caring for kittens and finding homes for them. In fact, a neutered pet can be a great joy to his or her owner. Nor does neutering a cat preclude the winning of prizes: there are classes for neuters and spays at all the championship shows, and Premier certificates to be won; three certificates, awarded by three different judges at three shows will make the cat, subject to the approval of the governing body concerned, a Premier; and then he or she will be able to compete in a class for Grand Premier.

Some years ago, I bred a British shorthair litter which comprised a nice Red Tabby male; a Scots lady wanted to buy him, provided his eyes were yellow; she intended to get two kittens, and to show them as neuters. I waited until, when he was four months old, I was able to assure her that Tangerine's eyes were indeed yellow, and she took him, and bought a charming Silver Tabby male of about the same age, and showed both kittens at the Scottish Cat Club's Show. They were exhibited in a mixed class, together, and they were both placed but Marcus, the Silver Tabby, was the better

kitten and was placed above Tangerine. Then disaster overtook
poor Marcus; he was caught in a trap and killed, and I felt so sorry
that his owner had lost the better of her two kittens. But as
Tangerine grew, his appearance improved; he developed a coat of
the most wonderful depth of colour, and he very soon became a
Premier. At one show, a well-known judge called to me to come and
see a cat with amazing coat-colour—and it was Tangye. In due
course, he became a Grand Premier, Premier Belhaven Tangerine,
and his local paper carried a headline 'Tangye does it again!' But
although he was a highly successful show neuter, he was also his
owner's loved pet, and he and she were happy together.

It is not always understood that it does a cat no harm to be
neutered. Some folk think it is unnatural and therefore wrong—but
the pact between man and cat requires that a pet cat shall be a
neuter. A short time ago a village family decided to keep a very
beautiful Cream shorthair male kitten, the son of their dark
Tortoiseshell, whose name was Chutney. He is so good-looking that
he is of show quality, and his owner wished to have him as a pet, but
her husband would not allow him to be neutered: in his view, this
would be wrong. However, fortunately, in due course he changed
his mind, for the next time Chutney was in season, her handsome
son coped with the situation, and this, their master thought, was
even more wrong, being incest; and so this cat has now been
neutered and he is very happy and very much loved.

Temperament

People who love cats are inclined to say that the breed of their
choice is exceptionally affectionate, sweet-tempered and amenable; however, when it comes to character, it can probably be said of
cats as of mankind that there are 'no two alike'. Of two cats living
together, one has been, all her long life, like Kipling's 'Lone cat who
walked by himself'—perfectly agreeable if caressed but never
seeking a lap, a wonderful mother, but preferring her cat-house to
the sitting-room. The other can never see a human being without
rushing to demand affection, purring like a dynamo and climbing to
the shoulders of people who do not necessarily want his
enthusiastic advances! Between these two characters there are
many degrees of friendliness: *Felis domesticus* is practically always
an androphile, and in every breed there are individuals who give

wonderful friendship to their owners.

Charles Darwin said of Manx cats that they 'differ from common cats in the want of a tail, greater height of hind legs, size of head and habits'.[1] Mrs Hellman says of these 'habits' that 'they are rather doglike in their closeness to their owners and like to accompany them on walks, usually talking the while in a quiet but persistent voice'.[2] She writes of her cats that they are good hunters, and that she had one cat who went into a pond after a moorhen, and caught it. An American lady, Mrs Charline Beane, who owns a Manx called Jubilation, relates that this cat kills rodents, but if he catches a bird he will carry it, soft-mouthed, to safety.

Cats as pets

For the pet cats, there is the danger of road accidents; and this is a constant anxiety for their owners. It has never been possible to legislate for the independent cat: he is almost as much free born as if he lived in the wild, and only very rarely will he submit to a collar and lead. Cats used for breeding are enclosed by their owners, but with present-day road conditions, a pet cat is at risk both in town and country. Fortunately there are many who are afraid of traffic and who, if they have a garden of their own, will not venture onto the road. There are not many with the amazing intelligence of the little black cat of years ago who belonged in Huntley and Palmers' premises in Reading, and could be seen on the opposite pavement, sitting looking at the traffic lights, ready to cross when they turned green.

In the very early days of cat shows, the exhibits were judged by size, and a really massive cat would be admired. Domestic shorthairs do, indeed, sometimes grow to a considerable size; I remember a Brown Tabby named Jim, a sweet-tempered, playful young cat with the fur on his 'waistcoat' spotted on a cream ground, who grew so big that he was considered too large for a town house, and went to live with some very nice country people. But Jim's size led to misfortune: he was shot dead by a neighbouring farmer, who mistook him for a young 'big cat'.

Most cats are philosophical travellers; in a good hamper or a regulation air-travel box, they will go to a new home or to a show without much fuss—maybe with none at all. Lady Haden-Guest, who is a well-known Governing Council judge, tells a tale of long ago when Maxim Litvinov who will be remembered as Russian ambassador to Britain before the first world war, was married to a cousin of the then Baron Haden-Guest; Litvinov was the Soviet Union's ambassador to the USA during the second world war, and he is thought of as a brilliant diplomatist, who was very popular in the West. His cleverness included bringing a present to London for his wife's cousin, seventy years or so ago; a present that he carried in the sacrosanct diplomatic bag: a beautiful, massive, pale-coated, thick-furred cat of good British Blue type! No wonder such an enterprising diplomat succeeded so well in making friends in the West! After all, quarantine laws were less stringent in 1910; and this cat evidently arrived in fine condition and none the worse for his journey.

Many famous people have had cats as pets, and the painter Turner had seven Manx in his house at one time! Where Manx are concerned there are as many legends as for Siamese, and they are no less apocryphal! Perhaps the best-known is the story of their arrival in the ark when, we are told, Noah accidentally shut their tails in the door!

Other famous people who have loved and protected the cat have been Louis XV of France, who liked the naturalist Buffon, and who owned a big white cat;[3] his queen, Marie Leczinska, also loved cats; a medal of this reign shows a big black cat,[4] decidedly a European, whereas Louis' white cat was a Persian, or Angora; the Angora figures on a lovely Sevres vase which was sent to the future Louis XVIII. In the next century, our own Queen Victoria owned a cat known as White Heather who, after her death, 'lived to a ripe old age in Buckingham Palace and died sincerely regretted by Edward VII'[5]

Sometimes the cats will have unusual friendships with other animals; I have seen good relations established between a family of woodpeckers and the cats who belonged in the garden where their tree stood on a big lawn. Often in summer the cats went under the tree for shade, and took no notice whatever of the woodpeckers, who walked on the grass pecking up grubs and ignored the cats completely; they seemed to recognise a situation of beak-versus-claws and to have agreed a non-aggression pact! Perhaps the oddest actual friendship I have seen was that between a young British neuter and a leveret; the leveret came into the garden through the fence that separated it from a big field beyond which there are woods; he started to run in a circle round the lawn and the cat, nearly full-grown, ran after him. They were much of size: a big, strong kitten and a young leveret; they chased each other and bumped into each other, and after a while the leveret stopped running and the cat put out a soft paw and patted his quarters to make him start playing again. They were half the morning together, and then the cat came indoors for his midday snack and the leveret disappeared. It was a curious friendship and a very short one: the leveret came back the next day, and the two young creatures chased each other in the sunshine—but that was the last time; he did not come a third time; it was just a passing encounter—but such a charming one!

I have had experience of two cats who were fine 'TV personalities' and they belonged to Australia and New Zealand. The first was a big kitten, a white Cornish Rex, who was the ideal creature for a broadcast. We were in Perth, in Western Australia; I sat in front of the cameras and answered questions about the cats, and I had this fine, co-operative little colleague on my lap: I held him up in front of my face and he looked calmly into the cameras—viewers must have seen a splendid picture of him! When I put him back on my knees, he settled down calmly until I had finished talking; he had never seen the studio before, nor any of the people in it, but he had the assured coolness of an experienced VIP.

My second television friend was a Manx. Miss Flavia Clifford-White organised a broadcast in Auckland, with four cats; no one was asking questions, so I talked about the cats, holding them up to the cameras; the Manx was splendidly co-operative: he stood on my shoulder, facing the same way as I did, and I turned my back to the cameras for a moment or two, so that his tailless end could be seen; he stood perfectly still, quite happy, and I was told later than the picture was a success—which was not surprising with such a sweet little collaborator.

Showing household pets

Most of the big shows in Britain and many abroad have classes for household pets with, very often, a celebrity to judge the cats: they are judged on condition, temperament, and conformity with their breed, in that order. Household pets are not, of course, always shorthairs; they may be of any breed, and often will be Siamese or

longhairs with no known pedigree. Of course, many people buy cats
with established pedigrees as pets to be neutered: as a rule,
breeders will sell as pets kittens who are not 'in championship
class', and will ask, of course, a lower price than would be expected
for a kitten with wonderful qualities to be exhibited and/or bred
from. Probably however, the majority of pet cats are shorthairs and
some are 'intermediate' longhairs.

The Oxford Cat Club caters exclusively for non-pedigree cats,
and holds an annual show, at which the exhibits are beautifully
presented (Chapter 8). Among this club's many activities is that of
giving advice when it is asked for and of teaching children how best
to care for their pet cats and kittens.

Feeding

The question of feeding cats is not really a difficult one: those
interested in show qualities frequently discuss various eatables
that will be suitable for the coats, or for keeping at bay any illnesses
that might affect their potential champions; but in fact, feeding cats
and kittens is largely a matter of common sense. Raw beef, raw
heart, raw liver, are all good for cats; liver should not be given in
large quantities nor too often, since it may be 'loosening'. If a cat
dislikes his food raw (this is rare but it can happen) then it must be
cooked for him. Cooked rabbit is good for cats, and so is plain boiled
or steamed fish. The enormous number of tinned foods marketed
for cats will do them no harm: but it is advisable to see that they get
fresh food, even if part of their diet comes out of a tin. The dry
foods, biscuits and so on, sold for cats are really good for them, good
for their teeth and good for their digestion; but it is a tragic mistake
to suppose that they can subsist on biscuit *only*. This might make
things easy for the owner, but it would starve the cat. Some notice
should be taken of the cats' likes and dislikes: many like
milk—quite a few do not. Water should always be available for
them. I have known many who were not interested in plain cow's
milk, but were quite pleased to lap up the cream from the top of the
bottle! Two good meals a day should be enough for a grown cat,
with perhaps a tit-bit at bedtime; kittens, who are growing, need
more frequent meals; and a queen in kitten, or feeding a family,
simply cannot be given too much too eat. A neuter should not be
overfed, though most pet cats persuade their owners to 'spoil' them.

It is really all a matter of common sense.

It is important to realise that there are possible dangers for cats in an ordinary household. There was a sad case of a young Rex cat who found a length of cellophane paper which had wrapped a steak and was steeped in blood; she swallowed the whole wrapping and an operation to remove it proved unsuccessful. This was a very well-fed queen—she was not hungry but was simply attracted by the blood. It is best, when cats have the run of the house, to be very careful in dealing with kitchen waste, for cats are greedy, and clever at finding things: most cats can open a pedal-bin quite easily; not by pressing the pedal, but simply by ramming the lid upward with a hard little head, and getting inside to investigate! So, it is advisable to wrap and remove to a firmly-lidded dustbin anything harmful such as bones or big lumps of gristle.

Cats and children

It ought, perhaps, to be said that if there are dangers for a pet cat, the cat may himself be a danger to a baby. Everyone knows, no doubt, that a cat will get into the cradle, pram or carrier, to curl up warmly with the baby; but it is commonly believed that the little one's life is at risk from a tendency of the cat to lie on his face; this is not, however, the real danger. The cat lies across the child's *chest*, and the infant pectoral muscles are unable to cope with the weight, so that the baby cannot breath—not because his mouth is covered, but because the cat is too heavy. Under surveillance of course, most cats are good companions for young children, and can be surprisingly patient.

A domestic cat, particularly a female, has usually a good understanding of the interests of young creatures, and will take great trouble to provide what is wanted. One queen, living in a cottage whose doors fastened with a latch, used to let her kittens into the sitting-room every morning: she simply climbed up the wooden, unpainted door to the rather high latch, and lifted it with her face; the door swung open, the queen jumped down, and the kittens streamed joyfully into what was evidently considered a desirable playroom.

The pet cat's intelligence with regard to her own little ones usually extends to the human babies: most adult cats understand that children have not the leathery, fur-growing epidermis of their own kind; they will realise that claws can hurt the thin, furless skin of a baby. A cat who does not sense this, or kittens, too young to know it, are better kept away from babies. By-and-large the pet cats are charming little friends and companions: going their own independent way, but always beautiful to see, exquisitely clean, and looking with friendly eyes at the people who care for them.

8

Character, Behaviour and Living Conditions

Today's breeders of fancy cats know well how the admired showbench qualities are inherited; the colours, the coats, the type of show cats are attributable to the action, usually mathematically predictable, of the genes concerned. It should be remembered that the genes control not only visible attributes, but also such characters as disposition and mental propensities.

Those who are fond of animals are apt to ascribe to their pets an intelligence so high that it would have, if it were indeed present, something of freakishness! 'He understands every word I say' is a common exaggeration; and owners of dogs and cats often claim for the particular breed of their choice an intellectual brilliance not, in the owner's view, present in other varieties. Plainly no cat understands 'every word'—he understands the tone of voice of his owner; he may find that 'Eats, boy!' shouted in cheerful tones, invariably means food, and he is quite sufficiently able to take care of himself to come running whenever he hears the familiar voice calling those words—but he could as easily have got used to a dinner-gong! In a paper sent to me by Mrs Jowett, who is a Tasmanian all-breed judge, Mrs Emery of Western Australia writes of her cat, Thomas John, a British Blue, 'When told to "go outside", he would do so, but sit patiently on the doorstep hoping that I would relent and let him stay. One had to say "right outside" and then he would go.... My cats would follow me wherever I went on the farm.' There are certainly degrees of intelligence!

Since nature's object is always survival, evolution produces in the species which have come from that original uni-cellular organism skills in obtaining sustenance: sabre teeth for the carnivore to pull down prey, beaks for birds, to excavate for worms, useful appendices for the herbivore, a fine sense of scent or hearing—a thousand and one adaptations. Man has domesticated many species, but only two, the dog and the cat, sought out man and recognised in him their best chance of survival. And it can be argued that of those two, the cat is by far the cleverer.

It may be said that for countless generations the cat has had everything he wanted from man, and has given nothing in return. This is of course, like most generalisations, not precisely true, for there are always two sides to a medal. There have been incidents of frightful cruelty when unfortunate malkins were burned with poor old women suspected of witchcraft, whose cats were said to be 'familiar' evil spirits. It is also a fact that the cat has helped man by keeping down vermin. Nevertheless, it remains true that the survival of the cat has for millennia been based on man's willingness to house and feed him.

Intelligence

When owners of shorthairs expatiate upon the particular intelligence of their cats, those who are well acquainted with all breeds will doubtless think that a cat is a cat with, from the angle of intelligence, nothing to choose between the moggie on the sidewalk and the champion pedigree cat. But there is a tiny grain of truth in what the shorthair's admirers say of his mentality: this is a very healthy breed. The cat has no speech centre in his brain, which is why his mind registers sounds but not particular words; he has not got the thick cortex that would make him capable of a long chain of reasoning; but he is capable of a measure of conceptual thought. As an example, for a queen to hide her young is instinctive—part of the in-built survival outfit that urges her to make sure no predator shall find them—but what of the queen who, in a shower of rain, picked up another queen's kitten from the wet grass and put him in shelter? Surely, this was at least an idea. And indeed, it can safely be said that the feline mind may be capable of a short chain of reasoning, and is certainly able to receive ideas.

In this, a strong shorthair has a head start over some breeds. He owes this to his perfect health, and this is due in part to his excellent natural physical conformation, and in part to the fact that he is not inbred. It is years now since a well-known vet.-surgeon told me that when folk asked her what breed of dog they should buy, she simply did not know how to advise them, since the favoured varieties of today have been bred sire to daughter and cousin to cousin until their breeds are ruined; she explained that man's insistence upon line breeding in order to perpetuate features approved in the show ring has produced animals of weak constitution, prone to such conditions as skin troubles, lacking in intelligence, no longer mentally alert, eventually stupid; and at last breeding with difficulty: a state of affairs leading in the end to sterility and death of the breed. Incidentally, a brother-sister mating probably holds more danger than the pairing of sire to daughter; for two sibs will carry *exactly* the same genes, which is not the case with father and daughter or mother and son. It is not necessary to be a qualified geneticist to know that individuals from a succession of like-to-like matings tend to be weak; what was told to me in respect of canines is true of all races. Any school-child knows what was the disastrous result in Europe of marriages in royal families between cousins: all the royal families were inter-related, and nobody not royal was thought sufficiently exalted to wed with kings and princes: the same genes passed on through generations perpetuated any poor characteristics, any unwanted recessives; the little Czarevitch was a hopeless haemophiliac, princes were mentally weak. The lesson to be drawn from this applies to cats. And man's interference has already harmed some show cats.

It is, maybe, a pity that people do not pay more attention to the immense store of common sense to be found in the Bible. We read 'he who will not work shall not eat', and we think vaguely that to do without dinner was a punishment to be meted out to lazy lay-abouts. But this is in fact a warning, and is exactly true: if, as a race, we do not till the ground and tend the cattle, we shall end without sustenance. Likewise, the injunction to a tribe living in a torrid climate not to eat pork was neither more nor less than good common sense. And common sense also is the clerical ruling which makes school children laugh: 'A man may not marry his grandmother' states the prayer-book. 'Whoever would want to?' shouts an irreverent infant, and his friends yell with mirth. But this instruction is headed 'Table of consanguinity', and consanguinity is the operative word. For the ancients spoke of 'mixing blood', never having heard of DNA. Even now, breeders of show cats talk about 'blood lines', and, alas, about 'fixing' some desired feature by a nearly-related mating.

But the strong shorthair cats, with their healthy bodies and alert minds, have always been outcrossed, and are not subject to the stupid, hazy mental processes which beset an organism whose forebears have been consistently inbred.

Behaviour

To get to know the feline character is to embark upon a most rewarding study; there is far more to the cat than just an animal who hunts mice and purrs when he is pleased. However, if it is true that a cat who is sound in body and mind will show intelligence, it is also true that in respect of our cats, anthropomorphism is an absurdity. To attribute to a cat the mental processes of a man is to make him appear ridiculous; to talk to him as if he were another human being is idiotic; the very word anthropomorphic was at one time used in a religious sense, and applied to man's tendency to 'make God in his own image'—a habit deplored by thoughtful persons who know that man exaggerates his own importance. And this exaggeration does, sometimes, make people talk to their cats as if they were an inferior form of man's own species.

Since we may suppose that the prehistoric cat was attracted to man's warm cave fires, and to the protection that these afforded against predators; and since man's rubbish dumps no doubt offered pickings and, maybe, attracted the ancestors of rats, who could, as far as the cat was concerned, be slain for snacks; and since this circumstance must have pleased man, as protecting his own food, a mutual tolerance was established. Cat was adapting nicely to a situation vital for his survival: he was, in fact, albeit by instinct, exploiting man. And all this time man's evolving brain was conquering his environment, and producing a way of life that suited his little camp-follower very well. All this is not an imaginative tale; the situation has not altered; from the compassionate cottager giving food to the stray whose little 'mew' sounds so plaintive, to the Thai aristocrat, Khunying Abhibal Rajamaitri, who likes to have Burmese and Siamese in her house, the process continues. Evolution has edged the cat into man's good graces, so that all the skills of the current 'dominant race' are available to him—and no tribute is exacted from him. Other animals are bred—and killed—for food for man; other animals, including the dog, are trained to work for man. The cat alone shares man's home, with all the advantages of man's knowledge of medicine, of preservation of food, and scientific protection against danger; nowadays even central heating is provided for a warmth-loving pet or a stud's outdoor quarters. And all the cat does is to exist beautifully. Surely, evolution has in effect made him the cleverest of creatures.

However, although much of the cat's behaviour is instinctive, and although it is stupid to attribute to him mental processes not proper to his species, still the cat is no fool, so that a good deal of intelligence can be found in such varieties as have not been weakened by mistakes in breeding made by man as selective agent; and domestic shorthairs, of all the show cats, measure up to this description. Two things are noteworthy in these cats and indeed, often in others—they are adept at getting their own way, and they are surprisingly observant. No cat is sure to settle happily in a given chair, basket or other place considered suitable by a loving owner. However attractive the arrangements made by the human slave, your cat is likely to leap away from the comfortable chair, basket or lap, if he is *put* there; it is quite likely that he will end up in the desirable venue, but only in his own good time.

Cats always know what they want. I know a queen who produced lovely healthy kittens, always in a tea-chest placed on its side and with suitable, old but clean blankets; the last time that she kittened, she was found by her faithful slave sitting in a basket in the cat-house, glaring at the tea-chest. The moment the chest was turned onto its side, almost without waiting for the blankets, she dived in with a little growl, presumably to mark her displeasure at the delay in providing the place where she wished to await her new family. They like their own way, and they know how to demand it!

Nor is there any doubt that they are observant: a cat knows the time; if you oversleep, he will wake you, always providing your awakening means that he will get something he wants; for if you are in the habit of opening the garden door for him first thing in the morning, he will have noticed the fact, and will insist upon what he has come to regard as his rights. Likewise with meals: he will have noted, if his owner is of punctual habits, the hours at which he can expect food—and if there is any delay, he will come and talk about it! Of course, since cats are not stupid, if the owner is away for a day his cats, though they will greet his return with demands for food, as well as with pleasure at seeing him, will not, despite their insistence that they are underprivileged, badly-treated creatures, be unduly disturbed by his absence: a healthy cat is inclined to be philosophical, but knows the time of day!

Although it is a mistake to attribute to any cat mental abilities that do not belong to his species, yet the statement that 'cats have a sixth sense' is very hard to refute. They know, minutes ahead, when a friend's car is approaching; before a man could possibly hear the sound of the car, or distinguish one of many engines of the same make, the sleeping cats wake, raise their heads, and look at their owner. Five minutes later, in comes the expected driver. This seems magical, but what is magic? Does this particular manifestation mean a sharpened sense of hearing such as that possessed by bees? Or is it a sort of thought-transference? Nothing is really 'uncanny' for nature does not transgress her own laws; nevertheless we have to admit there are times when some cats know something that their owners do not.

A feline skill that has no extra-sensory origin although it gives the effect of fairy-tale magic, is the cat's ability to vanish! What cat-owner has not observed that the arrival of visitors not approved by the cat produces a disappearance? The cat has definite likes and dislikes, and easily takes evasive action. What really happens is that he goes quietly to some place of his choosing: he may lie flat under the eiderdown on a favourite bed; or merge with a pile of sacks under a hot-house shelf in the vegetable garden. No amount of calling, no searching will find him. Yet, when the undesired visitor has gone, and the house is, in his view, back to normal, suddenly, without sound or apparent movement, there he is. It seems mysterious, but all it really amounts to is his skill in getting what he wants and avoiding what he dislikes!

Living conditions

It is not true that cats will take harm from inclement weather. They should be let out, even in snow, provided they can come running in when they want to — probably asking to be rubbed down, and not one whit the worse for an excursion into a white world.

It is true that a cat carefully enclosed and guarded against any possible infection can be easy prey for the first germ he meets if and when he does gain an hour of freedom. Nor is it sensible to treat a brood queen and her kittens as if they were hot-house plants. Breeders have been known to enclose the new litter and their dam in a fibreglass cage, artifically heated, and it is related that a queen will sometimes kill her kittens: the poor creature pads about with a kit in her mouth, seeking hopelessly for a way out of her too-small prison, and her teeth cut through the tiny neck, or the kitten suffocates. A parallel in human mediaeval history tells of Spanish princesses shut into their rooms, windows closed, for several weeks before the birth of their babies.

My own kittens are taken out on the second day of their lives, and put with their dam in an enclosure big enough to contain four dwarf apple-trees and a raised shelter; with a thick blanket, a soft cushion and a hot-water-bottle, the new arrivals are perfectly snug; the shelter's main door is closed and the queen comes and goes at will through a small, dog-kennel exit at the side. Of course, in weather that is bitterly cold or very rainy, no one would take them out, and they remain in their house, brick-built and adjoining the kitchen; one little room with their basket, tea-chest, blankets, hot-water-bottles—the other, through a slat, with their scratch-trays. But when they can, they go out: in good weather and after their eyes are open, their 'front door' is left wide and, after a while, they come out onto the grass and explore; and then they grow and start to climb the trees: delightful to watch! But all the time, the dam has the limited freedom of a very large enclosure, and always the small family is taken back to the cat-house before dusk.

It is, of course, good that kittens should be born in the spring—in Britain or the USA this means in March, April or May—so that they have the warm summer days in front of them in which to play and grow. And nature, always keen for the best chance of survival, has so arranged matters that a queen's most insistent call occurs at or soon after the winter solstice; normally her desire for a mate becomes intense after the shortest day, and supposing a January or February mating is arranged for her, then her kittens, born approximately 68 days after conception, will, when they arrive, have the good days before them. Of course, this is not a 'rule' and is liable to vary—but it is surprising how often it is possible to organise a mating that will lead to spring kittens.

Obviously, arrangements for new arrivals vary. With such a cat-house as my own, two litters of about the same age need one each of two rooms. This involves leaving a scratch-tray in the same room with the kittens: these rooms are big enough to have a place for scratch-trays behind a tea-chest; but it is best to tidy up reasonably frequently, for cats are immensely fastidious and queens do not like a scratch-tray too near their kittens. They will, or course, spend the daylight hours in their big, orchard enclosure. For those who have no garden, the matter of rearing young kittens is less easy; yet some arrangements can often be made. I know a cattery in Amsterdam where the owners' residence is a flat: but a flat with a most beautiful verandah, large, roofed and with netted windows, given over entirely to the cats. There is a small room at one end of this long, wide verandah which can be used for kittens, and there is a big glass door through which the cats come into the flat to be with their owners. They are not often enclosed in their own quarters — they even sleep with their humans; but when they must be shut in, they have every luxury and plenty of room and fresh air.

It is possible to buy pre-fabricated houses for stud cats and breeding queens; these are very well made by firms which have studied the question of feline requirements, and they can be installed in gardens where netted enclosures will make suitable runs for the cats, combining a measure of freedom with safety. Many breeders, particularly in Australia and New Zealand, make use of their own skills as carpenters or handymen to construct premises for their felines.

No one in the world has a more admirable way with the housing problem than an Aussie or a New Zealander; a usual attitude is: 'we buy a plot of land; we assemble materials and we build ourselves a house'. The houses are beautiful and have all possible refinements. I once visited some people who had a very large, sophisticated swimming pool; they said 'We have not quite completed it yet.' We may well wonder at such skills in folk who are not necessarily connected with the building profession, and who set about constructing an up-to-date residence as another might plant a small garden. And those who carry out such undertakings may also build splendid accommodation for their cats.

But there are still, unfortunately, people who keep their cats in cramped housing, not properly clean nor suitably warm. Mrs Pauline Stephens of South Australia, when she edited *Purr,* ran a series of articles headed 'Looking at Catteries'! In past issues of *Purr* can be found Pauline's views, her excellent advice and her descriptions of various catteries that she visited. In 1979, in describing Stirling Cattery in Western Australia, beautifully run by Christine and Peter Jol, she writes 'the welfare of the cat does not necessarily have to be sacrificed for the sake of safety...'.Sadly, she found, as she went the round of different catteries, that many outside runs were too small, and that there even existed owners to whom the cats were 'just breeding machines', and kept as if they were battery hens. Nevertheless, she visited many beautiful catteries, and in a letter she writes that her husband always says that 'in general the British keep their cats better than the Australians, and the Australians better than the Americans'. She adds, however, 'The most wonderful cattery I ever featured in *Purr* was an American cattery'. This was the Nepenthes Cattery, belonging to Joan and Alfred Westlhuber, and situated on the edge of San Francisco Harbour. These two people breed those charming show cats, the Abyssinians; but their splendidly organised cattery is, of course, a model home for any cat.

Mr and Mrs Westlhuber started with an advantage: he is an architect and she an interior designer. Joan writes: '…most of this property including our house and the cat house, is supported on pilings and extends over the water….. The security fences… enable our cats to have free access to the dock without being able to leave the property…? Here there are excellent kitchen facilities and bathroom accommodation, as well as suitable arrangements for queens and for stud cats, including the shelves and 'hidey holes' that cats love. Not everyone will be in a position to provide such magnificent housing. But any breeder should be able to give his cats proper food, warmth, and above all safety combined with freedom.

It is very important not to have too many breeding queens. Sometimes it is possible for a fancier to keep as many cats as he wishes. The late B. A. Stirling-Webb, for example, had big grounds round his large house, and he was in a position to provide a salary and a house on the premises for two ailurophiles whose work it was to look after his cats; he also spent a lot of his own time in caring for them, and thus he was able to keep quite a number of cats who all had everything they needed. Even today, there are fanciers who have families or friends living with them and interested in cats, so that it is possible for them to have quite a few, for if one person is ill or away, there will be others to care for the cattery. Some people have an arrangement with another ailurophile who will come and live with the cats while their owner is on holiday. But if you are a small family, or perhaps just a husband and wife, living in premises that are not particularly large, then it is as well to limit the number of felines. To keep a stud or a brood queen as they should be kept involves work. Proper food must be bought and prepared, every cat needs a daily grooming, blankets need washing and airing, scratch-trays must be well cleaned, floors must be scrubbed walls and doors wiped over: it is a chore. Given that you are young, it is still hard work. It is also expensive, for there will be a great deal to be spent on food, and a fair amount on running repairs: even if you can mend fencing yourself, you may need new baskets and the like. In addition, it is a lucky owner who never has any illness in his cattery, so that there may be some bills for veterinary attention as well as the cost of inoculation. If the kittens are to be sold, there will also be the cost of advertising them.

Boarding catteries

For many people there is also the question of holidays: it is a vexed one. You can find in the Fancy husbands and wives, both partners cat-lovers, who are seldom away from home and who are well organised in respect of the few days they spend on holiday. But many people regard an annual three weeks on a far-off island as a necessity, and for them too many cats may be a tragedy. A breeder with only a couple of breeding queens has trouble enough; for if the yearly exodus to the seaside is a 'must' then arrangements have to be made for the cats—and very likely for their kittens. Boarding catteries vary, even in this day and age. Fifty or 60 years ago, they were often disastrous: a means of making money, with the cats ill-fed and neglected, housed in a manner to allow any germ free play; run by folk who produced a lot of soft talk and, when the holidays were over, often said 'I'm sorry—the kittens were still-born…it happens sometimes…'.

It is not many years since a French friend told me a dreadful story of a cat she had put in a cattery in France; the unfortunate creature was locked into a cage far too small, and bashed herself to death against the wires without anyone coming to her rescue.

However, nowadays, it will be found that there is a number of boarding catteries run most efficiently, and with no chance of such a tragedy. It is common for such a cattery to have a row of cages, large, separate enclosures—a sort of terrace of suitable residences—built of wood and strong wire, and each with a big shelter that has shelves and inner compartments which no rain can reach. The 'houses' are wired for heating, for which an extra charge is made in winter. Obviously there must always be some chance of infection, though Mr Turner, of the superb quarantine cattery near Henley, told me recently a curious thing: if a cat should get some infection, it is possible for another at the far end of a different row of houses to contract the condition, while the next-door neighbours of the sick cat go free. This of course refers to some airborne condition, not to rabies, which is carried in the saliva and requires contact to infect another creature. To the layman, however, it is indeed curious that an airborne germ may pass by one individual to infect another much farther away.

Of course, if you are in charge of a boarding cattery you have the duty of keeping separate, sterilised feeding-bowls for each boarder; the cats' dishes cannot with safety be 'washed-up' all together in the sink. In addition, the cats must have separate scratch-trays whose contents have to be incinerated. In fact, it is not easy to run a good boarding cattery, and fees charged cannot be considered excessive. Those setting off on holiday, and who have no friends to care for their cats, will prefer to find a cattery near their homes; but there is one small thing that might influence choice: some boarding catteries are extremely bleak. The rows of perfectly-built houses are in a shady part of the grounds, scrubbed almost to the point of sterility, entirely adequate but spiritually chilly. Another cattery may have practically similar accommodation and yet be welcoming, producing a warm ambience for the little prisoners.

General care

The best advice for any breeder not having plenty of help with his cats is still not to keep too many. Often newcomers to the Fancy will love one breed—Blue longhair or Siamese, maybe, and stick to that breed alone. But some folk become fascinated by the different varieties of *Felis domesticus,* and these are the people who are in danger of overcrowding their catteries and making a chore of what should be a hobby. Anyone owning, say, a couple of Spotted Tabbies and a Rex, may see and fall in love with a Manx, and say 'I must have one! I must breed some!' Well—these cats are so very attractive that it would seem absurd to discourage anybody from adding one to his or her cattery; but unless there is plenty of help—maybe a whole family of cat-lovers—it is not a bad idea to wait; to decide that when one of the existing queens becomes too old for breeding, then a Manx shall take her place and she shall be spayed; or if there is already a friend who loves them to part with one and make room for an addition. An overcrowded cattery is not good for either owner or cats.

It is important to use ordinary commonsense in organising cats' meals. And it is always advisable to provide fresh, preferably raw, meat. Not everyone takes into account the matter of individual preferences: as in all living things, there are no two cats alike, and this applies to gastronomic likes and dislikes. Of two shorthair cats, mother and daughter, living together, one eats raw heart with enjoyment as well as raw liver and raw beef steak; the other will not touch heart; everything else is appreciated—the heart is left in the dish. Simply individual choice. Usually the cats like rabbit, chicken and fish; though fish is not, as so many people confidently declare, their natural diet: how would a cat in the wild ever catch a fish? Cow's milk, also, is not their natural drink—they could not in nature obtain it. It is very good for them if they like it, but it is extremely important to see that water is available for them—unless you have a cat who drinks a great deal of milk and refuses water, for that, also, can happen. By-and-large these cats drink plenty of water, and some of them have little use for milk—although the cream off the top may be another matter!

It is almost incredible that anyone should be so stupid as to make the statement that 'cats never break a leg'; but alas, there are plenty of people ready to make firm pronouncements upon matters of which they know nothing at all! There are many ways in which cats may break their bones, from those fractures sustained in a fall to an accident by contact with a car in the road. Fortunately, veterinary science can mend a fracture.

It is never of use to hit a cat. If he does something he ought not, and his owner gives him a blow, he simply will not understand why he has been hit. The proper way to show displeasure is the way his dam used: growl at him. At first sight this sounds absurd, but it is not, and it works. When a kitten misbehaves, maybe biting his mother too hard or, worse, mistaking the floor or the blanket for the scratch-tray, the queen will growl softly as she edges away from him or tries to tidy up; the kitten's ears will go down and he will look abashed. For the queen mistakes about scratch-trays are the ultimate sins; they hardly every happen, for the cat is the cleanest of animals and tiny kittens seem to have in-built knowledge of hygiene; but if there be a mistake the dam's displeasure, evinced in low, continuous growling, will be well understood by the kitten, whose expression shows clearly that he knows what it is all about. And if his owner wishes to indicate displeasure it is perfectly true that to growl softly at the offender will effectively show him that he has done wrong; it is, so to say, to speak to him in the language he understands; whereas a blow will make him angry and hurt, and he will not have the faintest idea why it has been delivered.

Truly, for those who are interested in him, there is more each day to be discovered about the cat, and to one who cares for him, the little shorthair, so long a part of man's household, will continually show new and fascinating facets.

9

Shows

Show management

Show management is probably the most difficult task in the Fancy. The stud-owner carries a heavy responsibility, for he is charged with the care of other peoples' queens and their safety and well-being; but the show manager's is a very big job, and it requires a great deal of knowledge and experience as well as a sense of responsibility.

Shows are run by the clubs, whose committees enlist the services of a show manager—often two nowadays, perhaps a husband-and-wife team. The visitor to the show sees a very big hall, with many exhibits in cages, nearly all in beautiful condition, with judges and stewards wearing overalls handling them or, in Europe and the USA, with stewards carrying them to a judging area; as the day progresses, officials will have put prize cards on the pens of the winners, and the visitor will be able to see the qualities that have impressed the judges. There will be side-tables with goods for sale: cat accessories of all kinds from carrying hampers to toys; books about cats; cat foods. The visitor will have paid an entrance-fee—a small one if he is a child or an old age pensioner—and he will find an award-board to tell him what cats have won; this he can compare with the catalogue that he will probably have bought at the entrance to the hall. There will be a platform with tables, and chairs occupied by officials dealing with judges' award-slips brought to them by stewards, various expense sheets, badges, championship certificates, and such small but important items as wire in case of a faulty cage; and, prepared to cope with endless queries and complaints, the show manager, apparently perfectly calm and always ready to make decisions and deal with difficulties.

For someone coming in because he likes cats, or just out of curiosity or a desire for entertainment, all this must seem a beautifully-organised 'Holy-of-Holies' for felines and those dedicated to their service. In the days of the Crystal Palace and the early beginnings of the Cat Fancy, a show was a very small affair for a few cat-lovers and their pets. Nowadays, hundreds—even thousands—of cats are exhibited and, in this age of 'more, bigger, swifter' undertakings, so many crowd in to see them that it is often difficult to move in the aisles between the pens. To the visitor who is new to the cat world, the lovely exhibits, the white-overalled officials, the rows of glittering trophies on the platform will be exciting and interesting; and the quiet, apparently unworried show managers must seem impressive figures. Some of the visitors will already know something about cats: perhaps will own a cat, or be interested in the idea of getting one—maybe even of becoming a breeder; such a person will be able to see the cats at close quarters, probably will talk to some of the owners, and begin to learn something of Fancy affairs. This kind of visitor will have some appreciation of the difficulties of running a show.

In fact, people who manage shows are dedicated to the work: no one who was not a lover of cats and all that concerns them could possibly run a successful show. The work of organising next year's exhibition begins as soon as this year's is over. The committee of the club concerned will decide upon its judges, and consult with its appointed show manager as to the hire of a hall; the matter of advertising the show; the schedule and the catalogue, the cost of printing; of hire of the hall; the letting of side tables, the selling of advertising space in the catalogue. There is the matter of arranging the trophies, of special prizes to be offered; the ordering of rosettes for the winners, and badges for officials. Judges must be engaged and accommodation booked for those staying overnight; the show manager will have endless letters to write; he or she will have to engage the services of vet.-surgeons to examine the cats on the day; to deal with entries to the show, sometimes from people who have not succeeded in filling in forms correctly. It may well be thought that the honorarium given by a club to its show manager cannot, in these difficult days, be commensurate with the work that has been done.

Of course, a show manager will have plenty of helpers; on the day of the show, the club's committee will take care of the trophies, the catalogues, the organisation of lunch for judges and stewards, and of the all-important award slips, which must go on the board for all too see, with copies sent to the governing body. So big have some

19 Grand Champion Tashmetum. Manx bred and owned by Mrs Hellman.
(Photo: Glen Hellman)

20 *Below* Supreme Grand Champion Tatleberry Long John. Manx bred by Mrs Hellman, owned by Mrs Audrey Jameson. (Photo: Marc Henrie)

21 *Right* British Tipped cat, owned by Mrs Brown. (Photo: Anne Cumbers)

22 *Top* Peerless Silver Jewel. British Tipped cat owned by Mrs Fawcett.

23 *Above* Rex kittens at play. (Photo: Derek Davis)

24 Cornish Rex kitten owned by Mrs Stennet. (Photo: Anne Cumbers)

25 Cornish Rex kittens owned by Mrs Stennet. (Photo: Anne Cumbers)

26 Nepenthes Cattery, San Francisco, USA, owned by Joan and Alfred Westlhuber. (Photo: by courtesy of the Editor of *Purr*)

all-breed shows become that there will be section-managers for longhairs, shorthairs and Siamese with, for instance at the National Cat Club's show, a show organiser (who has been for years now the splendidly capable Mrs Grace Pond) to direct all operations.

When the show is over and the cats have gone home, the pens must be stacked to be taken away, and the floor swept; and the work of seeing that awards are duly honoured, bills paid, debts collected and accounts accurately made-up and audited can start. It will take months to clear the paper work. The public, seeing the fairy-tale cats and the experienced manager and his helpers producing with apparent ease a delightful exhibition, very likely can have no idea of the enormous amount of work involved. The reward, for the show manager and his club and his committee, is the success of the show, and it is rooted in the love of cats. Most show managers will say that in the matter of expenses, which are enormous, they aim to 'break even'; it is not hoped to make a great profit, but only to ensure that there shall be no loss.

Rules and regulations

Those who enter their cats in a show can greatly assist the show manager and his committee by making sure that they really know the rules. Of course, some of the exhibits belong to fanciers of long standing who know all about procedure; but everyone must make a beginning, and many exhibitors are novices, people just starting as cat fanciers, who have perhaps bred a litter that they think worth showing, or bought a well-bred neuter who might become a premier; such folk could not be expected to know everything, though they may well be advised by a friend, perhaps the owner of the stud they have used, or the breeder of the queen that they bought. They will very greatly help the show manager if they carefully read the show rules and make sure that they adhere to them. To do this will also be a great help to themselves and to their exhibits. They will, presumably, have obtained a list of shows from a friend or from their governing body (in Britain, the Secretary of the Governing Council is Mrs Davis, see Chapter 9), or from their club. They will have chosen the show that best suits their exhibits, or that is easiest for travelling, and will have written to the show manager. They will receive from him a form to fill in, and printed copies of show rules, both the club's rules and the all-important governing body's rules. It is very important indeed to read and adhere to these rules, for not to keep them can lead only to muddles at best and disqualification at worst. Such rules will vary somewhat in detail in different countries; the USA, Australia, Europe, will have small differences in their regulations—and it is always necessary to know the rules of the country in which and the organisation under which you propose to exhibit. But the rules are based on the same principles, and it will be found by those who study them that those of the Governing Council in Britain are, like those of most countries, framed for the benefit and advantage of the exhibitors and, above all, of the cats.

Exhibitors in Britain will receive from a show manager the form to be filled in and a copy of the Governing Council show rules as well as the regulations of the club concerned, with full directions as to procedure. These last comprise all possible information as to fees, penning, conditions about the acceptance of entries, and advice for new exhibitors. Anyone reading these directions carefully can hardly go wrong in procedure.

The Governing Council rules are for the most part framed for the protection of the cats. They include the 14-day rule, whereby no cat or kitten may, within 14 days of appearing at a show, be exhibited at another show. This of course ensures that any infection that might be contracted at a show cannot be taken by an affected cat to another show. All exhibits are examined by a vet.-surgeon on arrival at the show hall; the relevant Council rule states that 'The decision of the examining veterinary surgeon...to reject an exhibit is final and no appeal can be entertained.'

Another Council rule states that 'Every exhibit must be provided with a sanitary tray and a clean plain white or near-white blanket without distinctive marking or edging.' This is to ensure that no judge shall know whose cat he is judging, and that no one shall say that the judge had some arrangement with the owner: this rule is a protection for the contestants and for the judges as well. A Council rule forbids the use of colouring matter or of anything that could alter an exhibit's appearance; and another forbids the use of powder on a cat's coat in the show hall.

'Exhibits which have been de-clawed will at once be disqualified'. Thus the Governing Council, and so it is under governing bodies in Australia and New Zealand and under some, but not all, the governing bodies in the USA (Chapter 6).

One of the Governing Council's latest rules concerns the question of a cat who bites a judge or steward; if a cat bites at three shows, he may not be shown again. This, of course, is quite right. But it is important to realise that a cat who bites a judge or a steward is not vicious: he is terrified. He has had a miserable, alarming journey in a hamper, away from the home where he has been a charming pet leading a happy life. He is in strange surroundings, a prisoner in a cage, with a lot of noise going on; the scent of many strange cats, of an unfamiliar place; with people he has never seen before, who come and start to take him from the dreadful little prison that is his only refuge in a nightmare world. Utterly panic-stricken, he retreats into the farthest corner, growling his terror, fighting against the threat of further horrors. He is not capable of appreciating the conciliatory note in the steward's voice, the hands that would hold him gently appear a clutching menace; frantic—he bites.

Of course, such a cat should not be shown again, for his own sake as well as for the sake of the people concerned. There are folk who are wonderful in handling a frightened exhibit: Madame Trayer, a distinguished French international judge, can fling open a cage door, pounce with both hands upon the occupant's back, and plonk him down onto the table to be inspected, all before he knows where he is. And Mr Richard Gebhardt of CFA has said that 'Any judge ought to be able to handle any cat'. I am very loth to disagree with so eminent an authority; but on this one thing I do disagree: probably because I have to admit that I cannot myself claim the ability to handle a really panic-stricken cat. I always tell my stewards 'If the cat says "No"—it's "No"'. Of course, a judge should return later to a cat who would not be handled; quite recently I judged a class of Siamese in which a cat—who looked like an obvious winner—said 'If you touch me, I'll bite'. This was disappointing but, half-an-hour later, he was much quieter; he allowed himself to be judged and he was indeed worthy of a challenge certificate.

It has to be remembered that equality is a human concept. We use the word as a kind of social gimmick, meaning that we are not willing to see one man exalted and another downtrodden. In nature there is no such thing as equality! As opposed to the absolutely panic-stricken cat, there is the one who, in a little time, becomes accustomed to his surroundings; and, at the far end of the scale,

there is the cat who enjoys shows. Such was Belhaven Nectarine, a
Red Rex that I bred years ago; he was the property of Mrs Alison
Ashford, who used to take him to shows and engage a double pen,
where he walked up and down at the front of the cage, observing
the people in the aisles and seeming to say 'Who's going to admire
me next?' Between the hopelessly frightened exhibit and the one
who thoroughly enjoys a show, there is a very wide range of
personalities! It is fair to say that the great majority of felines are
philosophical and take shows in their stride; the cat who is
hopelessly afraid is rare.

One of the Governing Council's rules runs 'Exhibitors are
forbidden to enter into conversation with any judge under whom
they are exhibiting until after the judge's engagement is completed.'
It is really up to the judge to refuse to talk to anyone not an official
until judging is over. And it is a steward's duty to protect his judge:
he must be sufficiently strong-minded to say with authority 'Don't
talk to my judge'. The rule exists, of course, to ensure that no judge
shall be distracted from his work by irrelevancies, or seem to be
persuaded by a friend to give an award to his cat: the exhibitor
could be telling the judge 'My cat is number so-and-so...' Judges
are very seldom indeed corrupt; this rule, however, is an insurance
against corruption and is also a protection for the judge; if no
exhibitors may speak to a judge, then no interested person, looking
down, maybe, from the gallery, can say 'He knows the judge—see if
he gets a prize for his cat...'. I once took a midday snack to a cat of
mine while Mrs Price, one of our Siamese judges, was starting on
his class; he was not of championship type, I was not hoping for a
prize and was exhibiting him only to show, in the early days of
Lilac-Pointed Siamese, the perfect colour of his points; when
judging was over, I apologised to Mrs Price who, gloriously sure of
her own integrity, said 'My dear, it would have made no difference!'

Nonetheless, there may be alarming incidents! I can remember a
nice man with, maybe, less than his share of intelligence, seizing me
by the shoulders as I went with my steward to a row of pens, and
exclaiming eagerly 'Oh, *Phyll!* You're just going to judge the class
my boy's in!' Well—the real trouble was that his boy was a cat of
extreme beauty, known to everyone, and practically certain to be
better than any contender. Like Mrs Price, I was sure of my own
integrity; but I could have done without the enthusiasm of the
excited owner! Since this cat was easily the best, he won his class,

but this was many years ago; I believe that nowadays it might, in such circumstances, be the judge's duty to disqualify the cat.

Thus it is of real importance for everyone concerned to read and know the rules. And the show rules and rules of governing bodies vary in different countries. It can be said that the rules in Britain, Europe and the USA are the same *in principle;* but they vary to a considerable extent in detail.

The Cat Fanciers' Association, the biggest governing body in the USA, has many rules in common with those in force in Britain; The CFA will, like the Council, not allow a de-clawed cat to win *any* award in a championship or premiership class; in the USA, also, shows comprise many rings. It may be possible, if a cat becomes the winner in one class, to transfer him, still at the same show, to another category for another class. But when it comes to procedural matters, there are strict rules governing such things as the entering of exhibits for different classes. In the USA judging is always conducted in a ring or area separate from the main hall; the exhibits are taken to the appropriate ring by stewards, placed in cages, and taken out by the judge, who washes over the table himself between exhibits, and replaces them when judged, fastening the awards on the cages. In Britain the judge goes with his steward and a trolley table to the cages in the main hall to handle the cats. It will be obvious that for exhibitors, judges and all concerned, it is necessary to know thoroughly the regulations for procedure of the country in which the show takes place.

It is essential in any country to abide by the rules of that country; a judge, for instance, should know the standards of the country in which he is officiating and should give them due weight, although he must not break the basic rules of his own governing body. In European countries the cats are judged in a separate room, and here again, show rules concerned with principle are no different from those obtaining in Britain or the USA; but matters of procedure vary, and so, for exhibitors, it is vital to read very carefully the rules for exhibition. The CFA's show rules are extensive and meticulous, and present no difficulties to anyone reading them carefully. In Australia and New Zealand, Governing Council rules are used, and the cats are judged, as in Britain, at their own pens. These rules also are easy to understand.

Judging in a ring has its advantages: in the countries where it prevails, the pens in the main hall may be decorated, since the public will see them but the judge, in a separate area, will not. In America and in Europe if a cat proves refractory, the judge may send for the owner to handle his own exhibit. Both in France and in Germany as well as in the Low Countries, cats who have won their Open classes may be put in a row of pens in the judging area, for the several judges concerned to decide which is the best-of-the-best.

South African shows

Mrs Linda Emery, South Africa's leading cat fancier, writes that there are plenty of shows in the Union: she herself is running three shows for two clubs in the Transvaal; but alas there is not much interest in domestic shorthairs in South Africa, where 'The ordinary man-in-the-street considers them to be just like the one next door and would...not be prepared to consider buying one.'[1] Evidently, cat-minded people in the Republic concentrate on cats of foreign type, but still, there are some pedigree domestic shorthairs and there are plenty of exhibitions so that maybe a vogue for them might grow.

The Rhodesian Cat Club, where Mrs Sylvia van Wyk is a prominent fancier, was organising a show in 1980 and they invited Mrs Emery to judge; but she thought that this would be a small show, since the country was politically troubled.

Australian shows

Shows in Australia are big, successful and beautifully run. I can remember a splendid exhibition in Sydney, where the show equipment included trolleys almost as long as operating tables, and where the aisles were quite wide enough to accommodate them. All these exhibitions, promoted world-wide, require the co-operation of the clubs and their governing bodies; of the breeders and exhibitors; of the visiting public; of show managers and their helpers and committees; and of the many groups of people whose interest is of help as stall-holders, manufacturers of pet foods and feline accessories, those who advertise in the catalogues, and the all-important vet.-surgeons who check the health of the contestants before they are admitted to the show hall. But of major importance, naturally, are the cats themselves.

Here, at the big championship shows, may be seen the cream of the Fancy—the very best of their breeds, all groomed to perfection. There is, too, international exchange of imported and exported cats; among the British shorthairs in the southern hemisphere will, for instance, probably be Brynbuboo cats, or some of their descendants. These strikingly successful show cats, bred by Mrs Absalom, have a world-wide reputation; Mr and Mrs Stephens, well-known judges in South Australia, imported two of them. Pauline Stephens writes that there is growing interest in shorthairs in Australia. She and Jack took their two imports from Britain, 'Huggy' and 'Betsy', to the Melbourne show, where they 'won nearly all the prizes'. She adds 'Jack took Huggy, our boy, to a big show in Sydney, where there were 17 British cats. Huggy was Best-in-Show..', that is, best of the shorthairs including Siamese. She adds 'It was you who told us that the Brynbuboos are the best... The first people here to take up British shorthairs were Mrs Jowett and her daughter in Tasmania....Their Blue male from England, Jezreel Jackpot, is a very nice cat who has done well at shows..'.

In Victoria, for 1979, the Shorthair Cat of the Year was a British Blue, Chanson Blue Royale, and the Shorthair Neuter of the Year was also a British Blue, Brooklea Beefeater. (I remember a truly wonderful Burmese called Creme Soufflé from the Brooklea cattery. 'Last January (1980) I judged a Blue-Cream owned by Brooklea Cattery who was very nice indeed'.[2])

It appears that Queensland is not as yet greatly interested in British shorthairs. In New South Wales, however, two ladies, Jeanette Ashworth and Janet Weir, who own the Aznaga Cattery, have a British Blue stud, Yowie Adrian, who is very good-looking indeed; and these ladies also breed Silver Tabbies, striped and spotted. Mrs Stephens was impressed by photographs of the British Tipped cats shown to her by Dr Groom, formerly chairman of the Governing Council, when he was in Australia. She says, however, that the breeding of Manx in Australia is not encouraged 'because of the health factor', but notes that she and Jack saw some magnificent Manx in the USA.

I am inclined to think that there are many breeders of Manx in America who, like those interested in them in Britain, select the best and strongest for breeding and achieve strong lines; if breeders never perpetuated Manx with long, narrow bodies, they would surely be as healthy as any other western shorthair. I can remember an amusing incident of very long ago when I was judging at a show in England where the exhibits in my classes were not very good; Mrs Earnshaw, herself a judge, was stewarding for me; and after some disappointing classes, I found in a side-class a magnificent Manx female. Knowing that Mrs Earnshaw was an expert on these cats I exclaimed 'At last! A really good cat—she *is* good, isn't she?' Mrs Earnshaw stared at me woodenly; I thought I must be wrong; her expression suggested it; she knew far more about Manx than I did. I still thought the cat was lovely and so, nervously, I put her up; and discovered afterwards that she was of my colleague's breeding! Mrs Earnshaw's blank expression had been assumed in order to avoid influencing me! However, this was not only a good-looker, but a strong, healthy cat, a fine example of what a Manx can and ought to be.

Mrs Stephens tells of the owners of the successful show cat Jezreel Jackpot that they have a truly patriotic prefix—Redwyton! It seems that British shorthairs are popular in Victoria, where their Shorthair Cat Club recently staged a show for British shorthairs and Abyssinians only; this show was, by all accounts, an outstanding success.

The British shorthairs are, of course, also bred and exhibited in New Zealand; and Australia and New Zealand have the advantage of being able to attend each others' shows and buy each others' cats.

Vetting in

One of the most important aspects of show procedure is 'vetting-in'—the inspection by experienced veterinary surgeons of each and every exhibit before he or she may enter the show hall. Attended by their stewards, the vet.-surgeons examine the exhibits and if there is anything wrong, the cat will be disqualified and removed; all schedules stress that from the vet.-surgeon's decision there can be no appeal. At the big championship shows, queues for 'vetting-in' may stretch half-way round the building, and exhibitors require a deal of patience. However, if you have pleasant neighbours in a queue, it can be agreeable to be able to exchange views and experiences with people who have the same interests.

Show temperament

The cats themselves are often far less frustrated at shows than are their owners! I can remember at the Royal Show Hall at Perth in Western Australia two cats of admirable temperament who were also good-lookers: champion Crystal Sweet Fanny, a Tortoiseshell of elegant type with wonderful eyes and magnificent whiskers, and a beautiful white Rex with a 'ripply' coat, both of whom were as calm as if they had been in their own gardens. And kittens, together in double pens, may be seen playing joyously—and sometimes making a hopeless shambles of their cage, scattering litter everywhere, rumpling their blankets, tearing white paper, and to crown all, upsetting their water-bowl over the lot. An owner, sent for by loud hailer to tidy the cage, must wonder if it is all worth it! He or she has doubtless taken endless trouble to present the little darlings to judges and public at their exquisite best: new, white blankets, small white drinking bowl, coats beautifully groomed, perhaps washed over with coatacine and then massaged with an expensive, genuine chamois leather, ears and eyes inspected, tallies neatly tied on with narrow white ribbon—not too loose, or they would get it into their mouths, and not too tightly for this would hurt. Grooming is, after all, important, though it is not, today, advisable to take the advice of Gordon Stables and 'touch her all over with a sponge dipped in fresh cream; when she licks herself the effect is wonderful.'[3] Still, the really conscientious owner, the ideal exhibitor, who has taken every care, must almost despair when confronted with healthy kittens conducting a mock battle on sopping wet blankets—and oh! how far a small amount of water can go!—with tallies lost or twisted to the back of the neck, litter everywhere, and pleased expressions on their faces!

Such minor disasters are not really very frequent, but perhaps they are the reason for a rule of the Cat Fanciers' Association in America that not more than two kittens may share a cage at shows run under CFA. Could it be that the committee concerned thought it best to give healthy kittens as little chance as possible to incite each other to riot?

Admittedly it is as pets that cats have their greatest charm: clean, quiet, beautiful to look at, purring and friendly, they are delightful in the households of those who like them. The loved kitten in a household of cat-minded people, the mouser in a cottage garden—they may well be happier than exotic creatures bred for profit; for there is no better life than that of a well-loved, well-cared-for domestic pet. And for anyone who enjoys competition—for children, maybe, who would like to see their pet taking part in important feline affairs—it is quite easy to join in the excitement of competing in a show, even if your cat is not an expensive, highly-bred feline, but a rescued stray.

Showing non-pedigree cats

Not everyone realises that it is possible for a cat with no known pedigree to appear at an important show; there are, in fact, classes for household pets at many championship shows worldwide. There was recently a charming household pet section, judged by a TV personality, at a very good show in Belfast run by the Ulster Cat Club; and many a show in Sweden has had a most attractive Husskattklass; the National Cat Club, at its very big show in London, has always catered for household pets: relevant sections will have classes for 'The cat with the biggest eyes', or for cats and kittens belonging to children, or for old age pensioners' cats, as well as those for black-and-white or for marmalade cats. The Governing Council's Show rule concerning exhibits and exhibitors reads 'Note 1—Show managements are entitled to offer classes for household pets.' There are, of course, no championships to be won in these classes, but many attractive prizes are offered in them.

Thus, a cat whose ancestry is not known may compete at a big show and, if he measures up to the requirements for the class in which he is entered, may be a winner. It is true to say that the exhibits in pet sections are frequently most beautifully presented—groomed to perfection and quite as worthy of the occasion as their well-connected cousins in the pedigree classes.

There is one club in Britain which caters exclusively for non-pedigree cats. This is the Oxford and District Cat Club, inaugurated in 1949 through the work of Mrs Ruffell, who had always given much of her time to the betterment of cats, and of Miss J. M. Eltenton, now president of the club. At the inaugural meeting was passed the resolution 'That an Oxford and District Cat Club be formed, the object of which shall be to foster interest in the cat, and to promote its general welfare, and to provide a centre for all local cat lovers.'[4]

This club's first show took place in 1953; there were only six classes. The show was for members' cats, and the exhibits were held on their owners' laps. It must have been reminiscent of the very early London and Birmingham shows, when everything was on so small a scale that show managers would meet cats at the railway station. The judge at the Oxford 1953 show was the late Miss Kit Wilson, a prominent delegate to the Governing Council who devoted her life to cats and to their welfare.

In the following year, there were pens for the Oxford Cat Club show, which from then on has been an annual event. Miss Wilson continued to judge for this club, and she had a wonderful way of explaining to children and others why their exhibits had—or had not—won prizes. Other Governing Council judges officiated as the numbers of classes grew, and a great many owners of pet cats brought exhibits. One year Lady Arkell, who lived in Wiltshire, said that she had brought her 'illegities' to the Oxford Show: they were the kittens of her Chocolate-Pointed Siamese queen who had escaped and mis-mated!

As the show grew bigger, classes for pedigree cats were added to the schedule, but the show at Oxford is always, as are all the club's activities, primarily for household pets. The aims of this club are to care for the cats and to advise their owners. The 25th of these shows was a Silver Jubilee show, at which every person present was given a special badge in commemoration of the occasion. There were some lovely exhibits, including pedigree cats belonging to members in a row of exhibition pens. The Best-in-Show of the competing cats was a longhair Tabby, a strong, healthy cat with a lovely head and eyes and beautiful patterning, a male neuter; the Best Shorthair was Mrs Hubbard's Uncle Poco, another male neuter, this time a Black-and-White Bi-colour with a lovely round head and a very good coat, who purred as if he were thoroughly enjoying the show. Perhaps the real highlight of the day was the row of decorated pens; they were beautifully, imaginatively arranged, and the judges present picked the best by ballot. It is true to say that no pedigree cat could be better presented nor more beautifully groomed than the majority of the exhibits that appear annually at this show.

Obviously, people who do not look after their cats properly are to be found, here, there and everywhere; at a recent championship show there was present a longhair who had great matted lumps of fur round his poor neck; such incidents highlight the importance of the Oxford club's willingness to help and advise all cat lovers. It is of great importance to present exhibits in household pet classes well-groomed and at their very best, just as it is if they are pedigree cats appearing in championship classes; for these cats are judged on condition and disposition and then on conformity to their breed. Probably the majority of cats exhibited in pet classes are shorthairs, but this is not a very big majority; quiet a lot of longhairs appear in household pet sections, and many of these are what used to be called 'intermediates'. This means that they have fur that is decidedly 'Persian' as opposed to short, but bears no resemblance to the tremendous pelage of the present-day exhibition longhair. It is an unsolved question whether the show longhairs were originally bred from cats brought from Ankara or Iran, or whether they are the result of selective breeding from the 'intermediates' which are native to the western cat population, and are probably simply a variation—with a coat of different length occurring in a predominantly short-haired population. These 'intermediates' were much prized by their owners in the early days of the century; people would say with pride 'He's got a *fluffy* coat!'

Surveys have from time to time been conducted, for instance to find the incidence of the prominent Black-and-White shorthair in various districts; but the provenance of the 'fluffy' cats does not seem to have been researched. It is obvious that the show longhairs have been bred not simply to perfection but to an exaggeration which sometimes seems a little alarming since it can lead to occlusion of the nasal ducts in an effort to broaden the face, and certainly produces a coat so heavy that the wearer seems in danger of being unable to move. It is not known if the cats with coats of intermediate length exhibited in pet classes are related to those imported from Persia and Turkey, or are simply individuals in the western cat population in whom a mutation has produced fur that is longer than that of the predominant shorthairs. Here are the views of a distinguished Australian geneticist, Mrs Mary Batten: 'It is known that there are polygenes which influence shorthair coat-length. These may also be present in longhair lines'. And 'It is arguable as to whether the 'fluffy' cat received its coat-length from the Persian or Iranian aristocrats or from the blending of cats brought from these areas by Romans, and the indigenous Scottish wild cat. However, almost certainly the factor which has produced the 'fluffy' coat is common to both sources. It is *not* an allele of either longhair or shorthair, but is a separate gene or polygenic series'.[5]

It is usual for a club in Britain holding its first show to be granted by the Council a licence for an Exemption Show, and then for a

Sanction Show, before it can be licensed to promote a Championship Show; thus an Exemption Show is an 'early beginning', and a Sanction Show is a 'dress rehearsal' for a Championship Show. The Shorthair Cat Society, however, distinguished for many years, was granted a Championship Show for its very first exhibition, held in 1970 after a long record of splendid work for the cats.[6]

A big show of today is almost a shopping-centre for cats! There will be stalls, not only for the benefit of feline charities, but for books, pictures, all sorts of cat accessories; if you buy a kitten at a show—you can also buy a hamper to carry your new friend, from one of the stalls. There are also tables taken by well-known manufacturers of cat foods; at the 1979 National Show at Olympia, Pedigree Pet Foods gave a party for the judges and officials after the show; they also gave presents of tins of their products to their guests.

In fact, a well-run show is a social occasion. And whereas it is true that sometimes a cat, rendered hopelessly nervous by crowds, is better not exhibited however good-looking, yet the big majority are perfectly philosophical, and many actually enjoy the excitement and the admiration. Mrs Hellman says of her latest Manx champion, Tatleberry Long John, that he 'walks along the Best-in-Show table like a professional model, looking at each of the judges as he goes past and posing beautifully for them...'.

10

Changes
Good and Bad

Change is one of life's concomitants—a part of the evolutionary process, and nothing 'stands still'; even a business undertaking must make a profit or a loss, must go forward or go back. It sometimes seems as though some of the reptiles, the crocodiles, for instance, have not altered since prehistoric times; but in fact, a close study will surely show a slow variation in any organism, and the word 'slow' is significant. Any alteration in the shorthair cat has been very slow indeed: he is not, today, very different from his ancestor of a century ago.

The rate of change is important. 'Evolution proceeds by a series of small, discontinuous variations'.[1] This applies to all species, from the meanest form of plant life to the cleverest race of men. And so far as the cat is concerned, the factors contributing to change in him are many of them due to the activities of man. The genetic alterations coming about through, perhaps, mutation, will not be rapid; but the proceedings of man will hasten the evolutionary process. It will not do, however, to think that the changes that affect the cat through man's interference are anything but natural: man's large-sized, reasoning brain is part of the overall evolutionary process, and when he uses it to produce and carry out the ideas peculiar to his species, he is simply fulfilling his evolutionary destiny; not, when he makes differences for, as an example, his cats, running counter to nature, but just obeying her behests and playing his little part in the tragi-comedy of her realm.

For the cat, some of the changes brought about by man's intervention are very good indeed, and some not so good. Clearly and without possibility of contradiction it can be stated that in the domains of medicine and hygiene man's science has very greatly benefited the feline race. Immunised against the diseases that once were a commonplace to him—including the horrors of rabies;

kept free of the parasites that beset him; protected from the results of infection by such discoveries as penicillin; and with any broken bones most skilfully mended: these things, new during the last 50 years, are changes that have enormous survival value for cats.

One of my neighbours has a splendid Red Tabby neuter shorthair who was hit by a truck roaring up a narrow footpath meant for pedestrians, and sustained a broken pelvis; only a few years ago this would have meant an unhappy death: now, duly plated and pinned, he climbs the trees and hunts the field mice. He is, incidentally, the son of a lovely shorthair Tortoiseshell who used to appear at parties wearing a small paper hat!

Sometimes patience is needed to listen to the views of ill-informed persons about feline illnesses! There are, alas, people who positively rejoice in the symptoms of illness. If they are cat fanciers, they acquire the little learning that is so dangerous, and they exaggerate what they have heard in the most extraordinary manner, sounding an alarm bell that arouses unnecessary fears.

It is right that someone sending his queen to a stud should want to know that he has been duly tested and immunised for panleucopenia, and right that a stud-owner should assure himself that visiting queens have received the protection available. Such precautions are reasonable, and to take them is to take good advantage of the changes for the better that have taken place. But we ought not to allow ourselves to think of these precautions as indicating that the whole cat population is riddled with disease!

The twentieth century is voracious in its demands for vast quantities of everything, for rapid alteration and for great speed. But speed is not in itself of value unless you are rushing to help someone or to get away from danger. And change may be good, or may be bad. For the cats, the wonderful scientific discoveries could not come into operation too quickly; but it is absurd to try and alter the excellent feline constitution to fit the new remedies! Those who delight in feline ailments produced, about three years ago, a tale about a condition known as luxating patella; this was said to be frequent in the Rex cat, though occurring in other breeds as well; and people—some of them quite prominent in the Fancy—described the misery caused to the cats by the affected knee-joints, and claimed to have seen many, particularly Rex, so affected. I had bred Rex since their debut in the '50s, and had handled cats of every breed all over the world for years, and I had never seen one case of luxating patella. So I asked acquaintances, who replied 'Oh *yes,* I've seen lots!' I am inclined to think that they believed what they said; but having been told of this condition, they attributed it to any cat seeming to crouch awkwardly. It was hard to accept that other judges had 'seen lots' and I had never seen a single one. Gradually, the words 'luxating patella' disappeared from cat-chatter; and a vet.-surgeon of repute has recently told me that the condition is a rare one: in many years of practice, she has seen one case of luxating patella, which occurred in a stray cat. Even the dreaded panleucopenia is not so common as rumour and exaggeration, quickly going the rounds, would have us believe.

It is of course a splendid thing that research for cats is being carried out at universities and special institutions; some of the best minds on both sides of the Atlantic are concerned with feline illnesses, and their findings have already saved a great many lives, and prevented much illness. It is a long time now since a vaccine was produced which is a safeguard against feline infectious enteritis, and research continues. It is, of course, vitally important for their owners to see that kittens are duly inoculated. During the lives of some of us cats were creatures who sometimes became sick, and it was not considered that anything could be done about it. Now, however, in this age of man's intensified searching into his surroundings, and making great strides in knowledge of all he can find, from magnetic fields billions of light years away to the behaviour of the genes of insects, modern morphology and technology in respect of *Felis domesticus* have not been neglected.

The findings of the researchers have helped many cats. But the writings of unqualified people have brought a measure of alarm and despondency to some cat owners. From the layman's viewpoint every year brings its crop of new and terrifying words describing hitherto undreamed-of conditions, not to speak of the names of all the new remedies. The uninformed owner of a kitten, interested in reading every periodical or pamphlet which has to do with cats, finds himself smothered in 'ias' and 'itises', all of which may affect his treasure, and in all the new 'ycins' that can be a cure. It is a splendid thing that biology and its allied sciences occupy themselves with feline troubles; but it is well to remember that many a cat goes through life with none of them.

Veterinary practice itself has changed in many ways over the years. It is not 50 years since I took a cat to be neutered at the surgery of a well-known and highly thought-of vet.-surgeon: the firm still exists, and is still of high repute, though the son of the founder, who was a schoolboy when I took my cat in for neutering, has now retired. The premises nowadays belong to the 1980s—not to the time when I took my cat along! I turned off the road into a wide, cobbled alleyway, leading to a smithy, and redolent of horses and harness with the occasional, at that time familiar, stamp of a hoof on the cobbles. There were small buildings, and I went into one of these, which was the waiting-room, and rang a bell. This waiting-room was small, and not very light, with a table in the centre and one or two sporting prints on the walls, and from an inner sanctum came an employee of the firm, a man of great expertise and no qualifications. I said sadly that I did not like anaesthetics for cats, but knew it was the law that you could not neuter a cat without anaesthesia once he was over six months old.

He took my large, handsome, well-grown Brown Tabby, stretched him out on the table, looked at him and said 'Mm—I shouldn't think he's six months! Wait a moment!' Into the holy-of-holies went my cat; about five minutes of silence; then this remarkable man re-appeared and said 'Here! You can take him home now! That'll be three-and-six.'

It is not yet half a century since I paid my three shillings and sixpence and took my perfectly contented cat home—but the changes that have rapidly altered all aspects of life are reflected not only in the enormous mass of veterinary knowledge which research has made available to cats, but in the aspect and ambiance of the veterinary premises of today. Over the question of in-patients, it 'can probably be said that the small-animal population are having increasingly improved facilities as the years go by'.[2] The register of the Royal College of Veterinary Surgeons has historical notes which take the practice of veterinary medicine back a long way: who reads about ancient Babylon or sees pictures of the ruins of Persepolis and thinks of veterinary medicine? Yet in the *Laws* of Hammurabi in 2100 B.C., the 'doctor of oxen and asses' is mentioned. A little more recently, Xenophon wrote a treatise on the horse; and one book in Aristotle's *Historia Animalium* expounds veterinary medicine.

The very interesting notes in the Register of the Royal College tell the story of veterinary practice in the British Isles from the fourteenth century, when vet.-surgeons were called Marshals; in the first half of the century the Master Marshals of London formed a guild, and an ordinance granted by the Mayor and Aldermen authorised them to practise their craft. Later, however, the art came to be practised by farriers, known as 'beast leeches', passing their recipes from father to son, and so fell into disrepute. It was not until towards the end of the eighteenth century that a Veterinary College was established in London, with a Frenchman, trained at Lyon, (where there was already a veterinary school) as its first professor: the Royal College owns, among other treasures, portraits of this M. de Saint Bel. A college was also established in Edinburgh by the famous William Dick, and these colleges were able to grant certificates of qualifications; but it was not until 1844 that a Royal Charter, granted to these two institutions, formed them into the Royal College of Veterinary Surgeons and declared the practice of veterinary medicine to be a profession.

Since then, there have been numerous Acts of Parliament concerning the profession; the first, in 1881, states 'It is expedient that provision be made to enable persons requiring the aid of a veterinary surgeon for the cure or prevention of diseases in, or injuries to horses and other animals, to distinguish between qualified and unqualified practitioners.' (Royal College Notes.) It is noteworthy that stress is laid on the horses—other animals are mentioned together. Horses were then of great importance to man— they were his means of transport—they came first. Cattle no doubt were also of great importance. Small animals, including the cat, were of lesser importance—expendable. Supply always follows demand. If humanity feels a need for anything, from face-powder to dentistry, the need will be exploited: it can mean money, and someone will decide to 'cash in on' the desires of his fellows; and then in the case of the professions will come those who will search and research for the love of it, seeking knowledge for its own sake. Thus, at the time when Frances Simpson wrote her book, the Cat Fancy was becoming a force, starting to be able to exert pressure, beginning to ask for assistance. Here was the demand; and the supply came gradually, with the beginnings of research which is now being undertaken at Bristol University and at the Morris Animal Foundation, after the great benefits conferred by the Sandoz Laboratories and Burroughs Wellcome; and with, in Britain, successive Acts of Parliament which protected cats as well as other animals.

Unqualified veterinary practice did not become illegal until 1949. The 1966 Act lays down that 'medical and dental practitioners may lawfully carry out or perform any treatment... upon an animal at the request of a registered veterinary surgeon...'. I well remember a kitten who had serious trouble with one eye, and was successfully operated upon by a very well-known oculist. In the 1966 Act also, are recognised degrees granted by the Universities of Melbourne, Queensland and Sidney (BVSC), the University of Guelph, Canada, (DVM) and the University of Pretoria (BV Sc.). The Royal College also may award a Fellowship, by examination or by thesis, or for meritorious contributions to learning or special eminence in veterinary science. The universities also grant higher degrees, and may appoint as honorary associates persons who have rendered services to the profession. The College Register has grown from its earliest list (1795) of seven men 'educated and instructed in every species of veterinary science' to its present long list, with worldwide associations.

It is certainly true that veterinary knowledge, in the early days, concerned itself principally with horses: in 1801 appeared James White's *The Anatomy and Physiology of the Horse's Foot.* The big animals received far more consideration than the little ones. But in due time, the profession came to embrace small animals—dogs, cats, birds and many others. This was partly because of the demand from owners of the small animals. In the last century, if a dog were ill, the vet.-surgeon knew how to put him out of his misery—his owner might sorrow for him, but his death was, after all, only to be expected. The sight of a dead cat in the road meant nothing much; there were plenty more cats. But as the nineteenth century faded into the twentieth, there came into being associations, such as the Royal Society for the Prevention of Cruelty to Animals, which were dedicated to their work; and there grew, from very small beginnings, starting in England and America, the Cat Fancy; so that veterinary surgery, with its practitioners beginning to concern themselves with the wider knowledge that has led to the great research institutions, began also to be asked to help cats whose owners wanted more for them than an easy way to the happy hunting grounds.

The headquarters of the Royal Veterinary College have been established in London, in Belgrave Square and Belgrave Mews.

Within living memory these mews were the homes of horses, who lived there with the grooms and coachmen who looked after them and the carriages which they drew; with the scent of harness and of the flowers grown by the coachmen's wives, they were like a piece of the not-so-far-off countryside come to Town. It is pleasant to think that these always attractive premises, built for the horses and, incidentally, occupied by a few well-nourished pet cats as well, are now part of the establishment which does so much for animals.

The word 'progress' is much used nowadays, and it is sometimes confused with 'change'. One of the dictionary meanings of 'progress' is given as 'advancement'; and certainly in the realm of medicine, the changes that have taken place have been advancement indeed—progress towards good. But for cats other changes have taken place besides those concerned with health, and they have not always been good.

Breeders of pedigree domestic shorthair cats can be heartily congratulated upon the fact that they have not sought to alter the appearance of their show cats. The poor Siamese, skimpy and narrow-jawed, the longhairs, short nosed and sometimes with occluded sinuses, have suffered through man's incomprehensible desire to alter their appearance. Such alterations arise from the wish to perpetuate and accentuate the features in the cats that are deemed attractive; the method is always the same one, based upon logic and commonsense; the original Persians tended to width of face, and this appealed to breeders, who chose the individuals with the widest facial contours to breed from, mating together the pair best conforming in this respect. Sometimes the lower jaws became weaker and the chins almost non-existent, so that the poor things, staggering under the weight of their exaggeratedly heavy pelage, had teeth that did not meet properly.

By great good fortune, what was admired in the domestic shorthair was his cobby body and his round head, his strong, thick legs, not too long, and his short tail. All these features were already present, and breeders have made no alterations in the type of these cats, but only in the matters of coat-colours and coat-patterns. It is true that the British shorthair and his European counterpart have, to judge from old pictures and photographs, a rounder head than had their ancestors of the early century; since the standard asks for a round head, it is clear that a breeder would select for such roundness; what is curious is that cats with no pedigree seem to have rounder heads than of yore—unless an escaped Siamese should intrude into their family tree! Ordinarily, however, heads, in Britain and France, seem to have an evolutionary trend towards round faces. In any case, the little western shorthairs have been lucky that in them no alterations in type have been attempted; for such changes may be retrogressive rather than progressive.

From Australia, recently, has come news of interference not beneficial to the domestic shorthairs. Mrs Batten has been asked for her views on the idea of crossing Manx with Scottish Folds. Such a notion can only have been prompted by love of change for its own sake and by the desire to meddle: such a cross could only produce a cat who looked like a freak—it would be a tragedy; these two breeds have already enough to contend with in refuting charges of peculiarity.

The second piece of news from down under is, if possible, even more disquieting. It comes from J.N. Stephens, the distinguished judge and breeder in South Australia, and it can best be described by quoting from the letter which he has sent to the Editors of several cat magazines in Australia:

> I have become considerably perturbed by the small size of some of the British Blues appearing on the show benches in the south eastern states, some so small that they can be described as petits, or even miniature. I became attracted to these cats in England because of their size and easy good manners....If this unfortunate tendency is not recognised and if this reduction in size of the British shorthairs in Australia is not reversed, the work of dedicated breeders during the last 100 years will be undone.

I have recently read an article in an Australian magazine, by an Australian writer, which could provide a clue to this trouble. She writes 'The British shorthair is a *medium* sized cat, not cobby ...' and also 'I can't think of a British shorthair as *massive* but, instead, muscular.'

The terms 'large', 'medium' and 'small' used by the Cat Fancy are, of course, relative.... After the first cat show, held at the Crystal Palace, London, in 1871, the *Illustrated London News* wrote an article on the show, illustrated by lithographic engravings of the six prize winning cats. One of these cats was a British shorthair Tabby and the caption read 'English cat, the biggest cat in the show'. This cat was probably the model which influenced the categorisation of breeds into large, medium and small.

Referring back to the Australian writer's description of the British shorthair as a medium sized cat, I must point out that the word 'medium' is nowhere used to describe British shorthairs in the official UK standards. The words relating to size used in the standard are 'powerful', 'well knit', 'deep broad chest', 'compact', 'short and strong legs'. The word *massive* is used in relation to the head, and if the head is massive, the body must be too, otherwise the cat would look completely out of balance...the words 'medium in size' are used in the official standards to describe the Siamese, and no one could believe that Siamese and British shorthairs should be similar in size.... I believe it is very important to the maintenance of a breed's quality to stick to the standard where it is specific. Tampering with the standard can have a most deleterious effect on the breed.... Unless the British Blue is recognised and bred as a *large* cat, it will lose the original features that make it so popular and also its reputation as one of the most eminent cats in the fancy.

This is a matter for great concern. It can be set right if the Fancy is alerted in time: the cats described by Jack Stephens do not measure up to the standard. If, however, the judges make very sure that they judge to the standard, then the miniature cats will receive no prizes, and disappointed owners will have to make clear to breeders that they will only buy cats that will be approved by the judges. It will be a tragedy, no less, if British Blue cats are to be miniaturised; and those who admire the strong British shorthairs may well be grateful to Mr Stephens for sounding the alarm.

Perhaps the greatest change in the situation of the cat is the change in his status: from being just an animal who attached himself to the kitchen in hopes of scraps, he has become a creature of importance: talked about, televised; his diet alone a whole industry. The domestic shorthair of the beginning of the century was just a hanger-on; the queens kittened where they might, and were lucky if they could keep one kitten; the rest were probably drowned—a most cruel death. Nowadays, factories work to produce special foods, suitable baskets, hampers, feeding-dishes, blankets—even beautifully-constructed houses for them as for all cats.

Thus change has, in the overall picture, greatly benefited the cats; and for the shorthairs of the west there have, so far, not been any deleterious alterations: they can be their sturdy, independent selves while graciously accepting the luxuries provided for them.

11

Associations, Journals and Institutions

Associations and clubs

During the last 50 years cats have been growing in popularity all over the world; and as feline affairs have become much discussed and of importance to ever greater numbers of people, so many services connected with them have come into being and grown from small beginnings into large undertakings. As in the early days of Empire trade followed the flag, so, during the present century, trades and professions are dealing more and more extensively with everything connected with cats: this is the measure of their increasing popularity.

First to serve the feline cause were the clubs and associations started at the end of the nineteenth century by the small band of people who bred and fostered the first 'pedigree' cats. A 'flyer', printed by the American Cat Association states 'The Cat Fancy in America had its formal beginning in 1897 with the forming of the Beresford Cat Club in Chicago. Named after Lady Marcus Beresford, founder of the Cat Club of England, the Beresford Club sponsored in 1899 one of the first cat shows to be held.'

So, the American Cat Association records the early beginnings of the Cat Fancy in the west, and describes how Lady Marcus Beresford and her friends in England and the United States inaugurated The Cat Club, which evolved into the Governing Council of the Cat Fancy and, in Chicago, the Beresford Cat Club, which is still today associated with the important American Cat Association, the oldest governing body in the United States.

The most important work of the new clubs and associations concerned registration. 'Also in 1899, the Beresford Club started the first American stud book on cats, and established the first American cat show rules. In 1904 some of the members of the Beresford Cat Club founded the American Cat Association, so that other cat clubs throughout the United States and Canada could share the common ties of an association and of a Stud Book Registry'.[1]

The value of registration cannot be overstressed. The Cat Club in England became in due course the Governing Council of the Cat Fancy; and besides the American Cat Association, as time passed eight other governing bodies were founded in the USA and one in Canada, and all of these have clubs affiliated to them; and the members all register their kittens with the governing body to which their club is affiliated. Thus there are complete records of show cats and their pedigrees from the inception of the registering bodies. This has great importance, not merely as a string of names of cats who have been well-known, but as demonstrating the breeding of the cats. If someone sends the appropriate fee to the secretary of a governing body, he will receive a copy of the pedigree of any cat registered with that body; and the pedigree will show not only any of the cat's forebears who have been champions or grand champions, but the breeds and colours of all his ancestors. The pedigree will, in fact, be an indication of whether the cat in question is 'pure' for this or that character and, perhaps most important of all, will be a guide to the likelihood of various characters appearing in the progeny.

Of course the governing bodies do other important work; the Governing Council has a Cat Care Committee which is of inestimable value in preventing ill-treatment of cats; the Cat Fanciers' Association, America's biggest governing body, produces a *Year Book* which is beautifully edited, and full of absolutely up-to-date information about the Fancy; the Council's Disciplinary Committee will hear complaints about any infringement of rules or unkindness to cats, and will deal with them. All these bodies may be approached by fanciers; the Secretary of the Governing Council is Mrs W. Davis, Dovefields, Petworth Road, Witley, Godalming, Surrey, GU8 5QW; and the Registrar for Shorthairs in Britain is (1980) Miss A. Rickson, 67 School Lane, Didsbury, Manchester 20.

It is often best for an individual to approach a governing body through his club; the club's officers will know whether it is advisable and possible to contact the governing body on a given matter; and if an affiliated club is prepared to put forward a proposition, and will perhaps do so through its delegate at a meeting of the governing body concerned, this will ensure a fair hearing. Whereas if the club is not prepared to back an individual request, its committee will make clear the reasons for not proceeding with the matter. Thus, plainly, an approach to the governing body is greatly strengthened if it is made through a club or society: in Britain, every club or association with a membership of a given number may be affiliated to the Governing Council and be represented on the Council by a delegate or, if the membership is very large, two delegates.

There are many clubs which deal with British shorthairs; for instance, in Britain, the Shorthair Cat Society, inaugurated in 1901; the Red, Cream and Tortie Club, dealing with both long and shorthair cats of this breed. In the southern hemisphere there are several governing bodies, including the Governing Council of the Cat Fancy, Australia and Victoria, which was founded in 1928, and the RAS Cat Club, Sydney. The former is the senior registering body in Australia; correspondence should be addressed to The Secretary, the GCCF Australia and Victoria, P.O. Box 73, Oakleigh, Victoria 3166.

Many clubs are affiliated to these and other governing bodies throughout Australia, and plenty of these are all-breed clubs. Catering particularly for shorthairs are the Siamese and Shorthair Cat Club, affiliated to the RAS; the Shorthair Cat Club, Victoria, affiliated to the Feline Control Council of Victoria; the Siamese and Shorthair Society of Queensland, affiliated to the Council of Federated Cat Clubs of Queensland.

In New Zealand, affiliated to The New Zealand Cat Fancy, are, catering for shorthairs exclusively, the Metropolitan Shorthair Cat Club, the Dominion Shorthaired Cat Club, Otago Siamese and Shorthair Pedigree Cat Club, and the Shorthair Cat Breeders' Association. All these clubs do a great deal for cats and their owners; I well remember the Siamese and Shorthair Society of Queensland's 1977 Show, at which the exhibits were of very high quality. And this society, in 1978, 'staged a show limited to British cats and Abyssinians which was a great success'.[2] In New Zealand, the Otago Shorthair Pedigree Cat Club, Dunedin, held a big show in April 1980. In America, CFA, founded in 1906, had an affiliated club in 1913: the Empire Cat Club; by 1978, there were, in the USA, Canada and Japan, 608 clubs affiliated to this, the biggest governing body in America, possibly in the world.

In Europe, many clubs are affiliated to FIFE—the Federation Internationale Feline d'Europe—and many are independent; in

France, for instance, the Cercle Félin holds shows in many districts, and the majority of European clubs cater for domestic shorthair cats as well as for longhairs, foreign shorthairs and Siamese.

It would serve no purpose to give a list of club secretaries, who are honorary workers; for a club may change its secretary, or the secretary may change his address; for anyone wanting to get in touch with a cat club, it is best to contact the governing body concerned, since such bodies will ensure the safety of their correspondence. The Governing Council in Britain, for instance, has as its secretary Mrs W. Davis, Dovefields, Petworth Road, Whitley, Godalming, Surrey, GU8 5QW, who may be written to for the following very useful lists:

Stud book	£10.00
Constitution of the GCCF	25
List of cat shows	25
List of affiliated clubs	25
List of judges	25
Standard of points	£1.00

These were the fees in 1980.

When writing for any of these, the appropriate fee should be enclosed, and any letter which requires a reply from the Secretary should be accompanied by a stamped, self-addressed envelope.

The Cat Fanciers' Association in New York has an office with a staff dealing with the all-important registrations, and correspondence may be addressed to the Editor of their beautifully produced *Year Book,* Marna Fogarty, at P.O. Box 430, Red Bank, N.J. 07701. This very big association has a board of directors who deal with many regions, and whose addresses and telephone numbers are given in the *Year Book.* Their President is the distinguished judge, Mr Richard Gebhardt, whose address is given as 77 Diamond Spring Road, Denville, N.J. 07834, telephone (201) 627-3108.

The best way for a novice to find out what he wants to know about the cat world is to join a club, contact his governing body, and attend cat shows; and an old hand keeps abreast of events in the same way—through his governing body and his club; if he attends club meetings, the club's delegate to the governing body will give a report of proceedings and decisions; and by the interesting discussions he may have with fellow ailurophiles at shows and meetings. Up-to-date information is always to be obtained from the press—not merely from the national newspaper and television reports on big shows in the capital, not only from local papers giving write-ups and pictures of local exhibitions, but from journals devoted to feline affairs.

Journals

In Britain, *Cats* has recently replaced *Fur & Feather* as the official publication of the Governing Council of the Cat Fancy. This good, colourful journal is published weekly, cost (1980) 35p, address: The Editor, *Cats,* Idle, Bradford, West Yorkshire, BD10 8NL. Here may be found information on Council affairs, sent in by the Council Secretary; judges' reports on championship shows; news of cat clubs, letters to the editor, and a wealth of up-to-date letters and articles concerning the Cat Fancy. Copies are on sale at newsagents, but most fanciers subscribe to this very valuable source of information. Besides its weekly journal, *Cats* also publishes an attractive annual, *Cats & Catdom.*

Monetary inflation (1980) has made the cost of paper, printing, and all the other adjuncts to publication almost prohibitive: *Cats* cannot afford to print such full reports of judges' comments on their classes at shows as *Fur & Feather* used to do; such difficulties coincide with an increase in the numbers of cats and exhibitions. These difficulties sometimes make it impossible to print reports except those on exhibits gaining first and second prizes, with none on winners of lesser awards. Thus exhibitors are often not able to read the judges' comments on their cats and kittens. These exhibitors do not, perhaps, realise that a judge is always happy to give information: the judge may be contacted by telephone, or written to—with a stamped envelope enclosed—and he or she will give a full report on an exhibit.

Most of the clubs have their own magazines, very often duplicated, and circulated among their members, to whom, naturally, they are of great interest. America has many journals which concern felines; perhaps the two best-known are the magazines, *All Cats* and *Cats,* both beautifully produced with excellent pictures, photographs and diagrams. Mrs Susie Page, well-known judge, author and breeder of Burmese and Siamese, writes for *Cats,* as she does for the *Siamese News Quarterly,* Sam Scheer's splendidly-edited journal for the Siamese Cat Society of

America. Mr Scheer has sent me a copy of *Cats Magazine* for March, 1980, and this periodical concerns any and every breed of cat. This particular number carries an article and lovely pictures describing a cat called a Safari, a cross between a domestic shorthair and a South American feral cat known as Geoffroy's cat, and belonging to the genus *Leopardus.* To judge from the pictures, one of them in full colour, and the description given by the writer, Patricia Hall Warren, the Safari strongly resembles the Spotted cat who is one of the domestic shorthair Tabbies (Chapter 8). This cross-bred cat has a great deal of patterning which includes many clear, distinct spots, and Mrs Warren describes the Safaris as '. . . Shorthairs. They wear a rich and specialised Spotted Tabby pattern of bars, dots, rosettes, face streaks, wavy stripes, leg bracelets and tail rings.'

In her description of the type of these cats Mrs Warren tells us that they have long bodies, but she also says that they are robust and that they have small ears. It appears that the Safaris have been crossed successfully with Siamese and also with North American shorthairs. It seems likely that the cross with a Spotted Tabby shorthair could produce beautiful kittens. And it is interesting to note that the progeny are fertile. The writer says that people believe that a hybrid must be infertile, but that this is not the case with feline hybrids. Of course, such a misunderstanding arises from the alteration in the meaning of the word 'hybrid' that has taken place recently. Language, like everything else, changes with the passage of time. Fifty years or so ago, 'hybrid' meant the result of a cross between two species, as a horse and a donkey—a mule, and infertile. Today, 'hybrid' means heterozygous: an organism carrying mixed genes. Thus a kitten born to a Rex cat mated with a domestic shorthair can be described as a 'Rex hybrid' meaning a shorthair heterozygous for Rex: i.e. carrying the gene for Rex. The parents of such kittens belong to the same species—both cats—and the kittens will not be infertile. Thus it is not really surprising that the Safaris are breeding, and they are obviously charming cats.

Down under there are many club journals, as for instance *Purr,* in southern Australia, edited by Pauline Stephens; and there is the excellent *Cats Australian Style,* which publishes an Annual in December: this publication is packed with information about all aspects of the Australian Cat Fancy, and is edited by Doug Reid,

P.O. Box 383, Elizabeth 5112, South Australia. Queensland has, among others, a very attractive magazine called *Catorama:* and another is named *New Zealand Cats,* edited by that very capable lady, Flavia Clifford-White; this is a very good 'glossy', with excellent photographs. Australia and New Zealand are in fact well-served by their 'cat press', and of course all such publications help to put people in touch, so that they can read not only of events but of the views of those with whom they share an absorbing interest.

Institutions

There are many organisations concerned with the welfare of cats. The Royal Society for the Prevention of Cruelty to Animals has long existed in Britain, and its inspectors are always ready to help any animal in distress; their aid is always forthcoming for cats who need it, and the Governing Council's Cat Care Committee— itself an institution existing to help cats—can always count upon the co-operation of the RSPCA. There is also the world-wide International Society for the Prevention of Cruelty to Animals, started in Scandinavia, Britain and the USA, and with its headquarters in Boston, Massachusetts.

Besides such big, international undertakings, many groups exist for the help and protection of the cat; the Cats' Protection League in Britain has been instrumental in countless rescues of ill-treated cats and kittens, and in saving vast numbers of strays. There are, alas, people who, having acquired a cat, later find him or her tiresome, and abandon the poor creature; in England, in an age when good education and civilized status is claimed for everyone, it has more than once or twice happened that a cat or kitten has been thrown from a car onto the road and left.

The Cats' Protection League will house rescued cats; its voluntary helpers and officials keep these strays in houses on their own premises, and feed and care for them until homes can be found. For anyone requiring a pet cat, it is surprising how often the CPL can supply exactly what is wanted: I was once asked if I could help an acquaintance to get a ginger cat, and I telephoned Mrs Irene Earnshaw, a Governing Council judge who houses CPL cats, and she had such a cat waiting for a home; he is a splendid creature and, now, a very happy one.

Those who, having no compassion, throw out a cat, have sometimes paid a high price for him: it is by no means unknown for the CPL and the RSPCA to rescue a pedigree Siamese or a show longhair; his owners will have paid a good price for what they consider a status symbol and, later, will have found caring for the cat a chore, and will simply get rid of him. Sometimes the 'status symbol' is a female, and is pregnant. People who will throw a queen onto the road from their car because they do not want kittens are not likely to pay to have her put to sleep. Why should they pay a vet.-surgeon's fees, necessarily high in days of inflation? Why, indeed, take the trouble to make an appointment, and drive to the surgery a creature in whom they have no further interest?

The cat, abandoned, pregnant, faces a life that beggars description. Indeed, the institutions for the safeguarding of animals are of great value. There is a true and charming tale of a little girl who wanted a kitten or young cat from the CPL, and was shown a row of pens where the homeless cats were housed; she looked at them all, and chose the dirtiest, scruffiest, skinniest kitten, so that she could take him home and make him happy.

Cats' Protection League helpers and officials are, naturally, careful to make sure that the poor strays go to suitable homes; they are handed over, 'free for nothing', to anybody who, though not well-off, will obviously care for their pet; but people who take a rescued cat and who are able to afford it, are asked to give a contribution to the League's work. Plainly, it costs a lot to house and feed the cats and to pay for veterinary attention for them; and those who take the little creatures into their homes are usually happy to contribute to the support of other homeless strays. The League's headquarters is at 20 North Street, Horsham, West Sussex, RH12 1BN. And an enquiry may be made there by people who want to know where to find their nearest associate of the Cats' Protection League. Addresses of RSPCA inspectors can be found in telephone directories.

Of course, there are various money-raising activities organised for the benefit of cat charities: well-wishers arrange, perhaps, a coffee morning with a bring-and-buy sale, and this can be an agreeable occasion for, maybe, elderly people who can spare a little time; such a small 'get-together' will give them the pleasure of discussing cats together, and will benefit the poor strays as well. Members of the CPL pay a small yearly subscription; and there will often be a CPL stall at a championship show.

To book a stall at a big championship show is, in fact, a very good way of promoting anything: pictures of cats; photographs; books about felines; pet foods; hampers and baskets and stropping-posts —those excellent 'mock-trees' so good for a cat's manicure, and so protective for the furniture! Visitors to a show will find that the stalls and tables round the walls constitute a sort of shopping-precinct for cats where may be bought anything from an expensive blanket to a bag of litter for the scratch-tray or a tea-towel with a feline design. An exhibitor, having forgotten some item of equipment, may almost certainly be able to remedy the oversight with purchases in the show hall.

Some of the stalls or tables are run for the benefit of cat charities. Indeed, charity is not always for the cats only; the hearts of cat-lovers are not concerned only with their animals: I remember a very successful show run by the Feline Association of South Australia for the benefit of an orphanage, so that the cats were helping the children, many of whom are often so eager to help the cats. This eagerness is fostered by the Oxford Cat Club, with its care for non-pedigree cats: here children are taught how to handle and care for cats and old-age pensioners are helped with their pets.

With so many welfare organisations and so much interest shown by clubs and committees, the cat is very well-served in these days, and he has the enormous advantage of the twentieth century's vast advance in medical knowledge: veterinary science, with its wonderful research centres, has advanced with all other branches of medicine. The small awareness of the beginning of the century has given place to a professional expertise whose field of knowledge is wide, and always expanding. Such knowledge is of great value to the small animals, of whom the cat is one.

Legislation concerning cats

It is a curious fact that the cat, by reason of his character, is virtually *ex legis*. The truth is that it is impossible to license, as in the case of the dog, an animal who cannot be caught and impounded and may quite possibly refuse to wear a collar. There are laws which protect the cat: it is the law that 'any person who ill-treats, beats, kicks, terrifies; carries or conveys in a manner likely to cause suffering to any cat; causes anyone to do these things; or being a cat-owner, allows someone else to do these things to his cat; is liable to a fine of up to £25, or to imprisonment... up to three months, or both'. Under British law a cat is 'larcenable' that is to say that anyone stealing a cat is liable to a fine of up to £100 and/or imprisonment.'

Cats are not easy to steal; as it would be difficult for a policeman to enforce the wearing of a collar (with name and address) if the cat were licensed, so it will be hard for a thief to get hold of a cat; but it has been done, usually by enticement, and for the terrible purpose of breeding numerous kittens so as to kill them, skin them, and sell their coats for fur as a commercial proposition. So, it is good to know that the cat can claim the protection of the law. The Police, the Royal Society and the various institutions will all help the cat if he is in trouble, and all may be appealed-to by owners of cats, who may be sure of assistance when there is genuine cause for anxiety.

The advantages that the cats receive from advanced veterinary medicine, from the protection afforded by the law, and through all the institutions and clubs inaugurated for them by people who love them are reflected in the beautiful condition of the show cats: those who really care for them will see that they get the full benefit of all that modern science and expertise can give them. And in no breed is this more evident than in the domestic shorthair.

In the household pet section for those with no pedigree, in championship classes for cats with distinguished recorded history, the little domestic shorthair cats are present in great beauty.

These cats were the witches' familiars, cruelly burned at the stake; the sometimes flea-ridden stable cats and mousers of more recent times. They are now presented at shows with their coats groomed to perfection; with ears and eyes perfectly clean since careful owners have obtained from the vet.-surgeon the means to deal with any suspicion of trouble; with their mouths in excellent order since any carious teeth will have been removed and any tartar will have been scaled. They will be contented with the attention they receive, for the cat is a very clean animal and appreciates all grooming. Their coats will not be so difficult to groom as is the overwhelming pelage of a show longhair; their fur will 'pay for' the attention it gets by its sheer beauty.

The domestic shorthair cat will always be a credit to those who take care of him. Provided with all the help that his owners can give him, properly fed and housed, naturally strong and healthy, may he live long with his human friends, and be as happy with them as they are happy with him.

References

Chapter 1

1. Letter to the author from M.N. Batten.
2. Heddon and Trengrove, *Wonders of Wildlife*.
3. Rudolph Brasch *et al., This is Australia*.
4. Letter to the author from A.G. Searle.
5. A.G. Searle, *Comparative Genetics of Coat-Colour in Mammals*.
6. Gordon Stables, *Cats*.
7. J. Bronowski, *The Ascent of Man*.
8. T.G. Field-Fisher, *Animals and the Law*.
9. Animals Act 1960 Section 1.
10. *CFA Year Book* 1978.

Chapter 2

1. Gordon Stables.
2. Khunying Rajamaitri.

Chapter 3

1. Letter to the author from M.N. Batten.
2. Ibid.

Chapter 4

1. Letter to the author from M.N. Batten.
2. Ibid.
3. A.C. Jude, *Cat Genetics*.
4. Letter to the author from Mrs Jane Hellman.

Chapter 5

1. A.G. Searle, *Coat Colour in Mammals*.
2. Pronouncement by FIFE in Sweden, quoted in the Hellman paper.
3. Hellman paper.
4. Letter from M.N. Batten.

Chapter 6

1. Lauder 1977.

Chapter 7

1. Hellman paper.
2. Letter from Mrs Hellman.
3. Nancy Mitford, *Madame de Pompadour* and *George IV and the Arts of France*. From the catalogue in the Queen's Gallery, Buckingham Palace. Cuttings sent to me by Miss Alannah Coleman.
4. From *The Life History and Magic of the Cat* by Dr Fernand Mery. Information from Miss Coleman.
5. Ibid.

Chapter 8

1. Letter from Mrs Pauline Stephens.
2. Notes by Mrs Joan Westlhuber reprinted from an article by Mrs Stephens in *Purr*, November 1978.

Chapter 9

1. Letter from Mrs Linda Emery.
2. Letter to author from Mrs Pauline Stephens.
3. Gordon Stables, *Cats*.
4. Oxford Cat Club brochure.
5. Letter from M.N. Batten.
6. Letter from Mrs Beaver, Chairman of the Short Hair Cat Society.

Chapter 10
1. Sir Arthur Keith.
2. Letter from John S.H. Morrish B.SC., M.R.C.V.S.

Chapter 11
1. ACA flyer.
2. Letter from Mrs Pauline Stephens.

Glossary

Agouti: The original wild-type mammalian coat-pattern with banded hairs of black, brown and yellow.

Ailurophile: Friendly towards cats. Noun: one who loves cats.

Allele: One gene of two or more at the same locus which have the same or differing phenotypic effects, being inherited from both parents.

Chromosomes: Cells existing in pairs and which make up living tissue.

Dilute: (of colour) Weaker, paler form.

DNA: Deoxyribo nucleic acid. One of the amino acids which forms the chain of life.

Dominant: Showing in the phenotype in the heterozygote.

Epidermis: Skin.

Epistatic: Masking the phenotypic effects of another, non-allelic gene; i.e. white, as the coat colour of a cat, may be a mask for another colour.

Eumelanin: Brown or black pigment.

F.I.E.: Feline infectious enteritis, a serious condition found in the cat and for which there is now an effective vaccine.

Gamete: The sex cell—the spermatozoon or the ovum.

Genic: Concerning genes.

Genetic: Concerning the science of heredity.

Genotype: The genetic make-up of an organism in respect of a given character.

Hydrophobia: The expression in man of rabies.

Melanocyte: The pigment cell.

Mutation: Change in the structure of heredity.

Onyxectomy: The surgical removal of finger or toe nails.

Ovum: The female reproduction cell—the egg.

Palaeolithic: Pertaining to the old stone age.

Panleucopenia: A condition of the bloodstream commonly known as feline infectious enteritis.

Pectoral: To do with the chest.

Pelage: Fur.

Pelvis: The bony cavity in the lower part of the abdomen.

Phenotype: The appearance of an organism in respect of a given character.

Phaeomelanin: Yellow or red pigment.

Pinna: The outer ear.

Polydactyly: The state of having extra digits. Greek: poly, many; dactyl, finger or toe. An extra toe or finger is not common, but it occurs, even in man, when amputation is usually performed in infancy.

Recessive: With no phenotypic effect in the heterozygote.

Sex-linkage: Attachment to one only of the sex chromosomes.

Spay: Noun — A neutered female cat. Verb — to neuter a female cat.

Spermatozoon: The male gamete.

Striations: Stripes.

Vaccine: A preparation made from dead or a-virulent disease germs and used as a protection against the disease concerned.

Vermicide: A preparation which kills internal parasites.

Vermifuge: A preparation which causes the rejection of internal parasites.

Zygote: Fertilised ovum with the diploid number of chromosomes restored.

Index